D1103994

Embolden Women:

Unapologetically Me

Rakshan Syed

Dedication

When it comes to women's empowerment, my dad Yousuf Mohammad is one of my most important role models. This book is a tribute to him. In his opinion, empowering his daughters and wife meant giving them the power and freedom to be themselves. He was a strong advocate of women actively representing all aspects of society and always having a voice in making key decisions. He did it without any discussion; it was second nature to him not to distinguish between daughters and sons, men and women.

It was honestly such a blessing to have a father who never questioned my desire to follow my heart. Instead, he supported me without any limitations. Regardless of the differences between my approach and the norm, he always backed my decisions. The unconditional support he provided for me, my sisters, and my mother is a true testament to women's empowerment. My beloved Abba, may God grant you the best place in Heaven! Aameen!

Acknowledgment

It is with great gratitude that I wish to thank my kids, Sarah and Umar, who were very patient with me during this time when I was busy writing the book and able to give less attention to their needs many evenings and weekends in a row. They have been the best kids a mom could ask for.

CONTENTS

About the Author

Rakshan Syed is the author of Embolden Women: Unapologetically Me. She is a mom, a career-oriented woman, and a daughter. Ever since she was a little girl, she has been passionate about women's empowerment. From a young age, she had a sense of unease regarding the universal acceptance of gender biases & would challenge the norms that would discriminate against women. She has a passion for women's education and career development. She strongly believes that every woman must be given equal opportunity in all facets of life. She is a Lawyer, Interior Designer, and a successful IT/Digital professional with a senior management position in a Fortune 100 company.

Her passion for women empowerment and gender equality is what prompted her to write her first book; "Embolden Women: Unapologetically Me". It's her dream to support women to be self-reliant, educated, and not shy away from the conversation. She has a firm belief that educated women make better choices for themselves and society, enabling and amplifying the voice of women in all facets of life where decisions are being made.

She is convinced women must be given the opportunity to be self-sufficient without depending on others, with full control of their life. She mentors and coaches women in her network and wants to reach a broader audience & help more women across the globe. For the global reach of her voice and message as a means of giving back to society, she started engaging with women via this book, enabling her to establish the platform globally.

Introduction

Ever since I was a little girl, I have always had a passion for women's empowerment. From a young age, I had a sense of unease regarding the universal acceptance of gender biases. For example, I wondered why our domestic help was always female, why there were no male teachers in my school, why there were no women's cricket teams anywhere in the world, and why men refused to change their own kids' diapers.

These recurring questions consumed me as I was growing up, and this curiosity was amplified by the fact that I almost felt alone in noticing these things. In fact, it seemed like I was the only one constantly noticing these differences, while everyone else around me seemed to either turn a blind eye or were comfortable with our expected gender roles and had no problem accepting things the way they were. I, however, was restless. It always felt like something was amiss.

"Embolden Women: Unapologetically Me"

I believe that this restlessness created a strong voice inside me for women's progression, justice, equality, courage, and self-efficacy. One day, as an eight-year-old growing up in 1980s India, I read an article in the newspaper about women being burnt in the name of dowry. It affected me deeply and made me question why society treats women not just different but, in such an inhumane manner.

A voice grew inside me which yearned to speak for the progress of women and the lack of overdue justice until finally, I found the courage to share this voice with my dad. I spoke to my father with conviction about my growing desire to do something about all the unjust and unfair treatment of women. He smiled and replied, saying, "yes, you could make a difference, but that will only be possible if you have the ability and knowledge to do so." These words stuck with me, and they have made an everlasting impression on me as I still feel their impact today. It might sound like a simple conversation between a father and his daughter, but his words emboldened me to be the woman I am today.

They gave me the courage to be Unapologetically Me, not in the sense of being unable to apologize, but in the sense of not having to apologize for being myself. Although I never had a singular goal to write this book, these words are a continuation of the conversation I had with my father and a further expression of my desire to make a difference for women everywhere.

Both my parents were very progressive for the relatively traditional times I grew up around in India and always encouraged their children, including myself and my sisters, to follow our hearts and passions in education, career, and life without any limitations. My childhood ambition was to become a lawyer so that I could try to help women and improve their plight. My father encouraged me to follow this path, and he discussed it with me all the time to assure himself that it was the right course for me.

As a result, he gave me wings to pursue my goal. In addition, my siblings and I were encouraged and supported by my parents to participate in extracurricular activities such as dance, sports, and debate competitions. As a student, my greatest passion was debate. I won every interschool debate I took part in. Back then, there were no computers, so you had to prepare by reading print media such as newspapers, magazines, books, or even through your own observations.

My dad would always find me articles about topics from different sources, challenge my arguments, and help me see the other side of the story. Life is much easier when your parents help you pursue your goals and ambitions because it allows you to be strong and determined enough to achieve them. I realized my goal of graduating from Bangalore University and earning my bar license. However, my plan to practice law in India changed when I moved with my husband to the U.S shortly after graduation.

When I came to the U.S in the late 90s, the IT industry was booming, and 'Information Systems and Services' was a definite buzzword. It piqued my interest, and after great consideration, I chose to pursue a Masters in Information Systems, landing me a career I am passionate about for the last 23 years. My legal background has contributed greatly to my career in information technology. My confidence, mental strength, courage, and my behavior are all a product of my upbringing and law school training.

The training I received at law school has enabled me to use rational decision-making and data to my advantage in all aspects of my career. Education continues to shape all of our lives, no matter what career or discipline we are in for the rest of our lives. It also helps develop your character and personality in the long run.

Writing this book is my way of providing guidance, influence, and inspiration to women of all ages who wish to break free from societal constraints and gender norms. My primary goal is to teach women to live life on their own terms, having the courage and confidence to not be controlled by other peoples' narrow perspectives. My mission is to enable women to deal with the consequences of their choices rather than let someone else take control of their lives.

My vision is to see women prioritize and put themselves first without having to feel guilty for it. Through this book, I aim to share tools and effective techniques for work-life balance, confidence, courage, and getting beyond tired, stereotypical views of women.

By empowering and encouraging women to value their unique skills, experiences, and voices, I hope to help them actualize the power to shape their own futures. In my own example, my greatest hope is to inspire young women to be their absolute best while navigating the pressures and expectations of society. I'm positive that you can do it, and all you need is a little push in the right direction.

For women, it is essential that we demonstrate strength and self-confidence while explicitly letting everyone know what we bring to the table. Inherently, women often hesitate to share their perspectives and explain why our contributions are relevant to the discussion. However, we should never deny ourselves the chance to contribute. The journey of my success in both life and career has had many twists and turns. There have been good and bad, and I have learned to treasure the good things and use them to inspire me to keep going on this path.

My children always hear me say that although there will always be negative things around us, there will also be positive things, so let's ignore the negative and focus on the positive. I would also like to shed light on how it's been my dream to support women to be self-reliant, educated, and confident during every conversation. I believe that when you are dependent on others, you are giving them more control of your life.

You can gain more control over your life if you take away others' ability to control it. If 50% of the population is shut off from contributing, we will not flourish as a society and will be unable to get rid of biases. Atrocities will continue to be committed toward women. Women need to be in every place where decisions are being made, and they must have a voice at the table. Think about it this way; if your voice is not heard, what's the point of having one? We need to empower women to own their identities and not underestimate their abilities. In a nutshell, we need to teach them to be "unapologetically me." I have been lucky enough to have supportive parents who gave me the utmost freedom to be myself, but that is not always the case for all. Numerous parents do not have a supportive attitude or mindset when it comes to their daughters.

They rather have broad and open-minded thinking for their sons. As a result, many women still struggle to have independence, ownership, confidence, and courage to face the challenges of life and work. I mentor and coach women in my network, but I also want to reach out to a broader audience and volunteer to help more women across the globe. I aspire to influence as many women as possible because we stand united and stronger together. As a way of enhancing the global reach of my voice and message and as a way of improving my contributions to society in general, I decided to write a book that would enable me to establish a global platform for women that would assist me in achieving that goal.

I'm very confident that the contents of this book are going to be life-changing, eye-opening, and revolutionary, to say the least. Not to mention, I'm certain that countless women will be able to realize and tap into their potential. I'm super excited to take you on this journey with me and hope to change the dynamics.

EMBOLDEN WOMEN

Help women to value their individuality, unique skills and voice in their future building.

MISSION

Teach women positive tools to navigate the pressures and expectations of society, and inspire every woman and girl to be their personal best in all aspects of their life.

VISION

Empower women to be unapologetically themselves without being controlled by mindsets.

VALUES

EMPOWER
TRUST
SUPPORT
RESPECT
INSPIRE
ENABLE
ELEVATE

STRATEGY

Create discussions, share blogs, mentor women and girls, develop workshops

LETS BUILD A BETTER FUTURE FOR WOMEN TOGETHER

"Embolden Women: Unapologetically Me"

Chapter 1: Managing Bias Through Emotional Intelligence

I have worked in engineering, information technology/digital for over 25 years. It's been a fascinating journey full of learning and immense growth. I began working in an industry where women were few and far between, let alone being in key leadership positions. At the time, I was not only one of the few women in this field but was also a woman of color and the first woman to wear a hijab at my place of work. But now, there are so many more.

It was no surprise that my family and friends discouraged me from wearing a hijab to an interview when I received a call for it. Unfortunately, because of my hijab, they thought I could not be hired in a traditionally male-dominated field. I shrugged off all the negative, discouraging comments and moved forward with a positive attitude, confidently believing in myself and taking pride in my identity. If I took off my hijab, I would be compromising on my identity, which was something I was never willing to do.

I was convinced that they would see past my dress code and focus on my competence for the job. To everyone's shock, they did. After all, there is always a light at the end of a dark tunnel; you just have to get through to shine. So, there was no stopping me from accepting the job and continuing this path for the next 25 years. I have encountered many frowns and raised eyebrows regarding my ambition to excel in my career without compromising my identity.

However, rather than getting discouraged, I used the experience as an opportunity to educate them on accepting diversity. My belief is that everything has a first time, so it was my chance to get them used to seeing my hijab as something that is not a limitation of my abilities but something that is an advantage and a personal choice. Neither am I different from anyone else wanting to pursue a career with ambition. It was not an easy journey for me; yes, it was uncomfortable, and I had to put in a lot of effort to be accepted by others. I'm sure everyone can relate to that at one point in their life.

I always felt extremely pressured to put my best foot forward and make everyone see beyond my dress code in all aspects of my life. In fact, people often had a different body language towards me, but I had to take the initiative and break the ice. It's unfortunate that women often have to walk the extra mile, go to extreme lengths to prove themselves, or even show their value.

Sometimes, it could also be because somebody's wearing a hijab, coming from a minority, or from an uncommon nationality. However, speaking from personal experience, self-efficacy, confidence, courage, a strong mind, and belief in your abilities will help you overcome any situation in life and make your mark. Confidence and a strong mind can undoubtedly be one of the biggest obstacles for women in the corporate world. If a woman brings more energy and strength than a man, she is perceived as aggressive and arrogant.

On the contrary, if the same is reflected from a man, he is perceived as charismatic, strong, and goal-oriented. The downside of this stereotypical expectation is that it limits many women's abilities, training them subconsciously to adapt to that unspoken expectation even when they are more capable than their male colleagues. Due to our acceptance of this bias, it continues and also ensures that sexist behavior will persist, making them believe they are entitled to this behavior.

In order to avoid reinforcing their bias subconsciously, it's high time we stop being vulnerable to their thinking. It is imperative that we, as a community, make a commitment to not limit ourselves, to have boundaries, be proud of who we are, be confident of our accomplishments, and welcome everyone around us to accept us and respect our differences. As a result, we will be able to form a welcoming and inclusive environment. Diversity and inclusion are about embracing various perspectives, especially if they differ significantly from our own. However, sometimes, we have unconscious biases that we remain completely unaware of.

Therefore, we must make more conscious efforts to become aware of how our unconscious biases may drive our behavior. If you find the root cause of a problem, the solution will appear seamlessly. Several years ago, I became more aware of my unconscious biases thanks to diversity and inclusion training.

I then realized that I was flawed in accepting diverse mindsets, although I genuinely thought I had accepted them on the surface. And sometimes, that's the thing; you need to look deeper into yourself to get the answers you're looking for. Perhaps my Indian roots contributed to my judgment based on mindset. Being Indians, we tend to differentiate ourselves from other cultures by thinking our way of living is better than theirs. Under the pretense of elite culture, we develop a low tolerance for diversity. As a general rule, I am convinced that people from different places have different pretensions. Nevertheless, this training spoke to me deeply. I sought to assess my attitudes toward diversity and identify any unconscious biases I might have.

Due to this experience, I made a conscious decision not to judge or be dismissive of others. Trust me when I say it really helped and gave me a new perspective as well. Nevertheless, accomplishing this was a task, to say the least; I had to remove my ego from my culture and background so that I could focus on people. People often refer to their ego as pride, but there is a thin line between pride and ego.

My mindset changed after putting people above culture and trends, allowing me to trust them more. By overcoming my own unconscious bias, I was able to break this barrier for myself, and this experience has enabled me to be a better person, colleague, leader, and mother. Stating the obvious, you can combat your own conscious and unconscious biases because you are in full control, but the million-dollar question is, how do you deal with people who have a bias against you? In a biased situation, there are two options: one is to be a victim, and the other is to fight.

I strongly believe that it is always better to fight back than to be a victim, as a victim mindset will only result in your destruction if you do not fight back. As a means of combating bias, we must express our views persistently and persuasively; we must challenge bias when we discover it and find innovative ways of moving forward. It is crucial that we constantly search for ways to improve diversity while not offending those who are biased against us in the process.

Providing constructive feedback is crucial to helping them understand diversity and inclusion. There is nothing more important than being passionate about your career and your success while also having a sense of pride as a woman who believes in empowering other people to help them succeed in life. Sitting on the sidelines and being a victim is easier than building the courage to challenge and learn, which is more rewarding.

When working on a project, you may have encountered situations where a friend, supervisor, or teacher is biased in their method and expects you to comply with their checklist. Next time you encounter these biases, challenge their inclusion. It will be a denial situation, but you must have a calm and inclusive discussion to get them to understand their bias. In my career, I've encountered a few people who truly believed they were the most inclusive because they accepted people from other cultures.

However, inclusion is more than just accepting people; it also branches out to enabling and accepting others who have different perspectives and ways of working. Regardless of gender, some managers are biased and highly resistant to inclusion. They possess a self-involved, egoistic, and dominant mindset thinking that everything is as they believe it to be. Thus, every time they're talking to people, they make assumptions. In my experience, such managers seem very harmonious and inclusive, but that's not the case.

In fact, it is the same individuals who are putting people in unnecessary boxes and determining whether or not others are capable based on their own ego-boosting attitudes, causing a barrier to the growth of others in the process. I guess we have all had to deal with people like that in our careers. I took advantage of one such personal experience to learn to be sensitive to different styles and approaches, not judging others based on my checklist of how they work with me.

Occasionally you can learn from the biases others have towards you, so you do not repeat them with another individual. It's important to learn from someone else's mistakes in a tough situation so you can become a better person, transforming the experience into a positive one. Thankfully, such experiences in my life have truly shaped me into a better person with a greater understanding of diversity and inclusion. The ease of dealing with bias when it is apparent and open is different from the difficulty of dealing with it when it is subtle and difficult to prove.

Only those going through it can see and feel it to know what's happening. Occasionally, you may also need to be subtle about it to decide whether the fight is worth your energy and time or whether it would be better utilized elsewhere. Having the courage for dialogue is another aspect that can't be undermined, so don't shy away from it. The importance of dialog goes beyond showing them how they can change but also enable you to maintain self-esteem, keep your head high, and believe in yourself.

We must learn to let go of toxic situations without suffocating ourselves with negativity or self-deprecation. It is critical that we do so proudly in the best way for our self-worth, self-esteem, and sense of belonging. Regardless of what path you have taken in life, subconscious bias will always be present. Our natural tendency is to flock to what we are familiar with. When we identify biases, both personally and professionally, we must continue to find effective ways and opportunities to overcome them.

If we seek these out, we will find allies along the way who will help us reach our goals. It is essential to identify them and be open-minded about capturing them so that we can make progress toward our goals without impeding our progress along the way. Some workplaces have leaders with traditional mindsets who embed a culture that does not appreciate and fails to acknowledge vocal, confident, and strong women in leadership roles.

Tradition-based mindset leaders don't like when women challenge them; they'd rather have women take a back seat. They are intimidated by strong, confident women who speak their minds. Here is an inspirational story of my little sister Rumana, today a senior vice president in a well-recognized bank, who faced a situation with a biased manager (direct supervisor) several years ago when she was a senior program manager. Her manager had issues with opinionated, strong women who executed without fear. She was leading a strategic project requiring several departments engagement.

He was not willing to accept she had better and broader knowledge than him. She was able to solve the problem that had been unresolved for two years in less than six months which didn't seem to go well with him. To his surprise, within a short time, she gained credibility within the organization across all the stakeholders and sponsors. She was recognized by the sponsor, stakeholders, and team members for the structure and governance she brought to the program and execution of her delivery.

He used subtle harassment tactics for her to quit the job. There were many days at times she came home emotionally hurt and exhausted. He would constantly criticize her every action and method irrespective of the stakeholders' and sponsors' appreciation of her work and execution. Almost without spelling it out, he wanted her out. So, he made it very hard for her to survive the job, which only made her more determined not to quit. My little sister, the fearless "unapologetic" one, did not succumb to his tactics and quit the job.

She challenged him for his actions & made sure her work spoke for who she was instead of his biases. She turned a project that was a failure for years into a great success in mere months. That caught the eyes of all the executive members, enabling her to establish a presence for herself in the organization. Imagine; if she had succumbed to that toxic manager at that time, she would never have been the strong leader that she is today. She did not try to appease or please him, nor did she try to fit into the boundaries established by him for being a woman.

She truly is an 'emboldened women' and knows how to be 'unapologetically herself.' I am so proud of my little sister for her passion and dedication toward her career, along with being a dedicated mother to her two kids. In an effort to fit in, some women try too hard not to draw attention to themselves, being afraid that their vocal presence will hinder their career growth. Thus, they stay quiet and take a back seat. But let me tell you, this is not the correct way to go about such situations.

"Embolden Women: Unapologetically Me"

We need to recognize that we are being judged differently because we are different. First of all, we are women, and second of all, we are women of color with strong voices and determination. Successful careers or successful lives require good listening skills, but it also requires courage to share your opinions, regardless of how different they are from the norm. Remember, all it takes is one small step to foster a big change, and it all starts with you.

By merely listening and not speaking, you are tainting the ability to utilize your true talents because you want to fit in. If you are pleasing criteria set by someone other than yourself, neither you nor the organization will benefit. Self-talk is extremely important; we must not let bias and their perceptions of us undermine our abilities. The truth is that we don't need to fit in; instead, we need to be true to who we are, and others must appreciate what we have to offer. If we become so occupied with trying to fit in, we will soon lose our individuality. I have learned from my life experiences that it is vital for women to indulge in positive self-talk and to believe in their abilities. We must ensure we don't let others' perceptions affect what makes us special.

The moment you walk away from the situation and examine how much it hurts to be rejected because you are different, you must know you have fallen into the trap of wanting to fit in. If you're having trouble accepting yourself for who you are, here's a tip to assist you: Get a piece of paper, write your USP (unique selling point) down or stand in front of the mirror and tell yourself what your USP is and trust me, you'll be astonished at what you realize.

When it comes to understanding emotional bias, it's also important to learn about emotional intelligence because it can help you better understand how to establish a connection with others. It teaches you how to handle conflict effectively and provides you with a new perspective of yourself, your surroundings, and your approach. Not to mention, it permits you to understand politics and biases around you and helps you see how your perception, as well as that of others, can impede your progress. Remember, the key to emotional intelligence is understanding a person's mindset or thought process in order to read beyond their words.

Having emotional intelligence means understanding, using, and positively managing your own emotions to relieve stress, communicate effectively, empathize with others, overcome challenges, and defuse conflict. Emotionally intelligent people fully understand how their emotions impact them and those around them. Therefore, emotional intelligence includes the ability to listen, reflect, assess, empathize, and regulate. If you aspire to be emotionally intelligent by reading this, it is essential to be self-aware and to self-regulate.

Self-awareness allows you to gain insight into how you feel and how it impacts others. As for self-regulation, you must learn how to control the way you react in any given situation, learn to stay calm and to not let your emotions get the best of you. The best part is that you can feel good about yourself regardless of the situation if you simply have the motivation to own and control the situation while remaining optimistic and maintaining empathy to understand the viewpoints of others and their body language.

Women are closely watched for flaws; this is readily apparent in the body language of those watching, especially when you are a woman of color or a minority. Suppose you want to break down this barrier. In this case, you first need to increase your emotional intelligence quotient by studying your audience, specifically those who convey subtle messages, with their body language, about their perception of you.

We tend to get defensive in our effort to respond to bias and prove our worth. Instead of being apologetic for who we are, we need to express our opinions and encourage them to see beyond our color, sex, or race with a discussion that cannot be ignored.

Techniques To Master:

Having a cheat code for a game makes winning

easier. Similarly, having certain techniques to help surpass the pressure of bias and defense will make the entire process simpler, less time-consuming, and more rewarding. Some of these techniques include using leading questions, reiterating our understanding of the problem/action, assessing our impact with suggested corrective actions, using the word 'we' more than 'I,' and making sure all are included in the decision-making process and holding everyone accountable.

Of course, you'll need the courage to overcome bias, but you'll also need emotional intelligence. In fact, both of them go hand in hand. Someone else's bias should not influence your behavior or approach. After all, your courage, emotional intelligence, and confidence should dictate the scene. People who doubted your abilities will then become appreciative of your abilities once you master this technique.

Acceptance is not an endorsement but an understanding that you can work with different mindsets even when their expectations and approach come into conflict with yours, and you become competent enough to succeed under situations like these. This is a vital step forward in leveraging diversity and inclusion in all its forms. Making people feel included is about making them feel welcomed regardless of conflicting mindsets and ideologies.

That art certainly leads to a better ability to deal with bias to a great extent. Learning emotional intelligence has enormously benefitted me in both my career and personal life. I have truly put my best foot forward to attain my goals, and I have full faith that you can do the same.

Key Takeaway:

First of all, we know that there generally is bias in society and that it's a lot more rampant against women. Secondly, all of us also carry some conscious and subconscious biases. Thirdly, emotional intelligence is important if you understand that you can also fight that subconscious bias or that you can deal with it better. The key takeaway of this chapter is that when you start identifying and dealing with bias, it improves intelligence. And when you start building your inclusion and diversity into the tango, because of understanding, you can represent yourself better and influence others too. This is one way to deal with those traditional, old-school mindsets and bring your confidence and strength to the table along with this.

Take my word for it; the above-mentioned is a brilliant tool that you can utilize. It's important to keep in mind that your confidence and strength are going to help you recognize what is on the table. Moreover, it also helps you have a prosperous career in two ways, one is influencing others, but the other is teaching yourself how to deal with it. All in all, it's a win-win situation.

"Embolden Women: Unapologetically Me"

Chapter 2: Fighting a Mindset

As a woman, do you sometimes feel that you put more effort into pleasing others and meeting their expectations rather than utilizing your strengths and focusing on your own needs and expectations? If that is the case, then take my word for it; you're definitely not alone. Thousands of women feel the same way on a regular basis but what matters at the end of the day is what you choose to do about it.

It's time to ask yourself if there is something greater and more meaningful than yourself, something you want to change to avoid becoming a slave to someone else's perception or mindset. Challenging them takes a great deal of courage as it allows them to see things from a different perspective than they have ever had, particularly if their mindsets are male-dominated and if they believe it is best for them. As long as mankind has existed, a male-dominated mindset has ruled every part of our lives, which is the biggest hindrance to women's progress.

I'm so heartbroken and disappointed that the supreme court overturned Roe V. Wade. It is a shame that America has stepped backward in time by denying women the right to make decisions about their bodies, as if they didn't belong to them, treating women like an object owned by a man, government, or state.

So much for all that has been accomplished in the past 100 years in terms of the equality of women. One more thing contributing to the objectification of women is that a woman's body is not her own but everyone's. An action such as this will have devastating consequences, and it must serve as a wake-up call for the young, especially women. Unfortunately, we have not learned from history. Society, men, organizations, and governments make these decisions for women, putting millions of women's health at risk.

This is a perfect example of how fighting a mindset is harder than fighting an individual mind. Throughout history, women have been strategically controlled to think like men by man-made laws and rules under the guise of values, norms, religions, customs, cultures, etc. As a result, at times, women think acting like their traditional male mentors is appropriate behavior. Sadly, instead of uplifting and supporting other women, they sometimes become obstacles to other women's success without realizing it.

To sum it up, those women, in particular, are subconsciously mimicking a controlled mindset without being aware of their own identity. Therefore, women empowerment needs to acknowledge who was at the table, writing those rules, and then challenge them so that we can close the gender gap in society. "Fighting the mindset is a bigger challenge than fighting the minds." We need to carefully examine how each of us can combat the mindset from every angle in our society. Women at all leves need to become ambassadors for each other so that we can learn to "Be Unapologetic" and "Embolden" each other. Then, and only then, will women have a truly unapologetic moment when they will be able to speak their minds without fear of consequence, whether at work or at home?

To achieve that, we must first eliminate the unconscious bias embedded in women's role-play. There are many cultures in the world where women have a clearly defined role to play, so much so that if they violate that role, they are questioned and challenged by their women matriarchs before the patriarchs of the family can even step in. As a result of generations of enslavement and cultural norms, women are not even aware of the violations they've been subjected to for generations while accepting the status quo.

Due to this, there will be a long wait before you see any sort of change. Here, you are fighting more mindsets than minds. In today's so-called progressive urban society, stand-up comedians that employ sexist remarks against women in the name of humor have become a major source of entertainment. Don't you think that's just pathetic? Women who question this are called uptight, prudent, killjoys, etc., not just by men but also by other women because of the "normalization trap."

Normalization is the process through which ideas and actions come to be accepted as 'normal' and seem 'natural' in everyday life. The harsh reality is that we are caged by the normalization trap when society accepts wrong behavior in the name of normality, such as prejudice, misogyny, or violations of human rights. I want you to open your eyes and realize that there is widespread manipulation and exploitation being done under the word 'normalization.'

Men often think of women as objects after falling victim to this normalization trap. They make inappropriate remarks about them without any remorse. Additionally, women's silence subtly commends this behavior as they have subconsciously accepted man's dominant position over their perceptions for generations. When we choose to let such things slip by, we are adding to the problem. In fact, we are part of the problem. Remember that silence often speaks volumes and can give the wrong notion about you being comfortable with things that are not appropriate. Although, I don't think that silence is entirely a woman's fault because it's a result of several years of manipulation and brainwashing. It is now, more than ever, essential to educate women about the normalization trap that prevents them from progressing in society.

The fact is that society is actually terrified of women progressing and rising above the standards and limitations set upon them. Thus, it ensures women are kept in a vicious and eternal cycle of suppression. Most of society's rules are set by men and endorsed by past generations of women who were taught that these values are true regardless of race, religion, or culture. I say, take it as a challenge, do not underestimate the opportunity to recognize a normalization trap when you see one. I encourage all of you to be advocates for fighting the mindset and questioning things at the root level. By doing so, we may be able to eliminate the gender gap and discrimination as we progress toward a progressive society.

Before you proceed to the next chapter, please take a moment and reflect upon your last week; identify times when you were caught in the normalization trap and ways to overcome it. I assure you; that the sense of empowerment will be profound. Fighting a mindset is always more challenging than fighting the mind because "Mindset" is an "established set of attitudes typical of a particular group; the outlook, philosophy, or values of an individual; generally, a frame of mind, attitude, or disposition."

A mindset is typically a fixed state of mind. A change of mind is easy, but a change of mindset is much more complex, especially if you have deeply ingrained cultural beliefs. The longer we hold on to a belief, the harder it is to change it because it becomes a part of who we are. But just because it is difficult doesn't mean you can't fight it or challenge it.

"Embolden Women: Unapologetically Me"

In today's technologically advanced world, women are still excluded from education, job roles, dialogue, and even seats at the table because of the mindset. We need to strive and maximize every opportunity to combat the mindset that prevents women from being a part of society on an equal footing. In order to dismantle the entire system of inequality, women must gain power in corporations, education, politics, culture, and society. If we don't start now, we may never succeed in our mission.

Here is a story of how persisting in fighting a mindset can pay off if you are persistent. My mother-in-law was a great inspiration when it came to fighting the mindset. She was born in India in the late 1930s and grew up in a conservative environment; where women's education was not prioritized. Traditionally, people believed that women were meant to raise children and that education did not yield value. Instead, it was considered a waste of money. In addition, going to school in those days was a bit of a challenge due to transport limitations. Moreover, there were no schools in neighborhoods beyond middle school.

Many people had to travel away from their neighborhoods to get a high school or college education, and women traveling long distances were looked down upon because they were away from home for long hours of the day. Additionally, the cost of education for women was not acceptable to many families, regardless of their financial standing.

A passion for education was incredibly uncommon for a woman at that time and place, causing many to raise their eyebrows. They did not value her goals and dreams, claiming them to be a nuisance. However, she chose not to pay any heed to those things; her focus was unshakable. She made sure to chase her dreams, follow her mind, listen to her heart, and ignore everyone else as if they were just background noise.

Her mother died when she was very young, and by the time she was a teenager, she had also lost her father. Growing up, she lived in a joint family who did not value education for any gender, let alone support women's education. Yet, despite all the odds and cultural clashes against women's education, she received her degree in economics, became a college professor, and wrote a book for non-English speakers. Her battle against the mindset was truly a great example of how to break down barriers.

Women's empowerment is exemplified by her ability to fight cultural beliefs and norms in order to achieve what she believed was her right. This was her "Unapologetically Me" moment when she did not give in to the constraints of the society that was trying to hold her back. Each time she described her experiences and struggles to achieve her educational goals, her passion for education was evident.

She negotiated every step along the way to achieve her education goals, dealing with illiterate, old-school mindsets to make them see things her way. Her top priority was to earn scholarships throughout her undergraduate studies so that her relatives wouldn't be burdened and wouldn't force her to stop going to school. Throughout high school, the fear of losing her scholarship motivated her to excel academically in order to secure a scholarship.

Imagine having such a great passion that she pursued her education despite all of the difficulties. Imagine how difficult that must be for a teenager; to deal with not only the emotional turmoil but also the financial burden and still stay focused on her passion for pursuing her higher education. I think that's truly commendable.

She was a great example of women's empowerment through education and empowered many, irrespective of gender, with her encouragement and support for education. Throughout her life, she never missed an opportunity to support the cause of education by giving charity, guidance, and advice to the younger generation. If you know the cultural system for the women of India, specifically at that time, you can appreciate the struggle she overcame to become an educated woman.

In my opinion, there is no better example of a woman fighting a mindset than this. I know that reading this is pretty inspiring, but it's imperative not to let that inspiration fade away after you feel inspired. Similar to how my mother-in-law stood her ground, strived to educate herself, break stereotypes and fulfill her dreams, you have the power and ability to do the same.

Back in the day, there weren't as many resources or technological advancements as we have today. If we begin utilizing our resources, expand our minds, and filter the things we have been taught for centuries, we can have our own unapologetic moment. Over the years, I have learned that all it takes is a few seconds of courage, and once you get used to living fearlessly, you don't allow yourself to be controlled like a mere puppet.

Key Takeaway:

Fighting a mindset will cost you sweat and blood, but you won't regret it once you decide to take the plunge. Taking the first step is usually scary but starting somewhere is necessary. The change you're seeking won't happen overnight, it will take a long time, but if you persist through the storm, you will eventually see the sunshine. Rome wasn't built in a day, either.

It could be months or even years, for that matter. I want you to always remember that nothing is impossible, even if you have been taught that some things just can't be done. My mother-in-law made the so-called 'impossible' possible back in the day and succeeded in her mission only because she believed she could. Your beliefs greatly impact how far you can go in life, so don't let the negative ones restrict you.

Be positive, think well, and act on it at the right time. When I'm mentoring other women, this is something I say to them, also. Thinking about doing something is one thing, but devising an action plan to act upon it is another thing entirely. Stay focused and determined. Always believe in your power and potential to attain the things that you wish for. Don't let anyone tell you that you can't do something; anything is possible if you have the will and put your mind to it!

"Embolden Women: Unapologetically Me"

Chapter 3: Start, Stop, Continue

Subconscious bias exists in various situations and among people all around us. We must constantly look for ways to eliminate our subconscious bias in every situation. Before discrediting people for their weaknesses, we should use facts and data but also err on the side of caution before rejecting them due to their weaknesses. The key is to shift your focus to people's strengths instead of their weaknesses.

In fact, when I put this theory into practice, I became a better leader, friend, mother, and colleague, which was also the beginning of my journey towards agile and lean leadership. I've come to realize; it's not people but the culture that fails people, and blaming them is the worst thing you can do as a leader. I have spent a lot of time building my brand as a lean and agile leader.

I am a strong believer in the value of lean and agile leadership for female leaders. That was a prominent chapter in my life when I began to think beyond the framework more in terms of culture. I realized how vital it is to the entirety of your life. It's all about the people not suffering at the hands of culture. If you look closely, you will evidently see how culture has successfully shaped us, our thoughts, and our behaviors in a negative light.

The problem persists because **people don't even view it as an issue**. Incorrect things are taught and ingrained in our minds under the impression of them being part and parcel of culture. However, this is not true. I first learned about Agile methodologies and Lean management in 2009. My passion for business agility was totally in line with agile values. In simple layman's terms, Agile refers to continuous incremental improvement through small and frequent delivery. There are four main values according to the Agile Manifesto, which are as follows:

1. Individuals and interactions over processes and tools.
2. Working software over comprehensive documentation.
3. Customer collaboration over contract negotiation.
4. Responding to change over following a plan.

Even though Agile is primarily used for software development, I believe we can apply it to all things that need to progress and grow. My mantra in all aspects of life has been and still is to deliver the most value in the shortest amount of time. A key element of an agile business is rapid decision-making, and that mindset prompted me to seek out agile work environments.

An agile mindset allows you to be honest with your people, provide transparency regarding the problem you are trying to solve, set realistic expectations for the team, and clarify the changes you need to make. When you look closely at the four agile values, you will find that they are focused on people working together, being able to collaborate, negotiate, and manage change.

Similarly, people, collaboration, negotiation, and change make society better. As you become more acquainted with the framework, you will realize how Agile is primarily about people. Developing an agile mindset starts with thinking agilely in every way, and I believe that agile thinking starts with thinking about people first. Influencing people is my greatest passion, and if you can make someone successful, everything else falls into place. Agile leadership is a great tool for working mothers and women in positions of management.

To get great results, you have to trust your people, appreciate them, encourage them, motivate them and empower them to do their best. Trust, in my opinion, is the most important element in building a positive relationship. Without trust, you will have nothing and no one to work on, either. In order to achieve agility, everyone must work together in harmony. Imagine if our society was built using agile methodologies, no one would suffer indifference or injustice.

But unfortunately, our society doesn't operate on this methodology. As a matter of fact, it aims to have the masterminds feed their ego and build the rules and principles at the cost of others, especially those different from them. A person's degree of comfort with changing environments is determined by whether it is difficult to adjust to change or whether it is easy for them to do so. It is essential that you are comfortable with change and willing to embrace it.

Change is inevitable, so embrace it. In life and at work, you can't succeed without trying; to try something new, you have to be willing to fail and learn from it. If you fall down seven times, stand up on the eighth time. Don't let a previous setback stop or discourage you from trying again with the same amount of determination. The fear of failure is known to stifle your ability to innovate and change. You can accomplish something by thinking big, starting small, learning, and taking corrective action when you fail. Society must learn from its failure to acknowledge the role of women as equals and contributors to society at every level and iteratively identify pathways to empower women in every aspect of their lives.

Let's leverage the "Start, Stop, and Continue" retrospective practice used by agile for women's empowerment which is as follows:

Start giving women the same opportunities as men in every aspect of life.

Stop the disparity in pay between men and women.

Continue to be rigorous in the empowerment of women.

Whenever I think about agile and lean mindsets, I am compelled to challenge society to recognize the failure to launch women as male equals and to respect their intellect and ability to be at the forefront of every aspect of society, no matter what they do in politics, corporations, education, or sports. We can all be agents of change and apply those principles to stop the culture and mindset from failing women.

Let's figure out how to provide the best value to women in the shortest possible time frame. To make this happen, each one of us must be the change agent, willing to keep trying until we succeed. We will only be prosperous when we stop talking about this and start acting. It's about creating a high-performing culture that celebrates women daily. Without further ado, here are my ideas for empowering women, and you can add yours to this list to be that influencer for women's empowerment to leverage every opportunity.

Ideas/Ways of empowering women:

1. Mentor high school and middle school girls to lead the change by challenging their mindsets, so they are prepared for the world.
2. Organize community development activities and workshops to make local women aware of the importance of self-reliance.
3. Share your stories by utilizing platforms like TED talk and podcasts to share even the simplest

achievement as a woman. By doing so, thousands of women across the world will feel inspired.

4. Celebrate women's successes and failures in moving towards self-empowerment through blogs and articles.

5. Become an advocate for other women in the workplace, encouraging them and sharing your experiences with them.

6. Do not underestimate the importance of a shift in culture for women's advancement.

7. From an early age, start teaching daughters the self-confidence and courage to stand up for their values with self-efficacy.

8. Be a cheerleader and supporter of women whenever you can.

9. Take small steps since they can make a big difference; empowerment doesn't need a big boom.

10. Women's empowerment involves giving them the freedom to 'be.'

11. Allow women the freedom of speech instead of suppressing their voices. They need to be heard and let it out.

Key Takeaway:

In my opinion, women should work hard to defeat the subconscious bias that exists and also spread awareness of it by making others realize how they are projecting it. Society needs to embrace women with agility and educate its people about an agile mindset to truly flourish as a whole. Not to mention that another aspect that can be worked upon is letting go of the anxiety/fear of failure.

You need to embrace yourself and believe in your abilities. It is important not to let go of your willingness to try and change and learn from failures. Instead of thinking of the wrong women will do once given the empowerment they rightfully deserve, why not think about what they will do right once they have that opportunity?

We must alter our mindsets and think/speak from a logical perspective rather than blindly being led by the blind themselves.

"Embolden Women: Unapologetically Me"

Chapter 4: Women of Substance-Breaking Barriers

Parents play a crucial role in helping daughters become confident and courageous. They are the first pillar that can teach them to be "unapologetically themselves." As parents, we must be aware of the cultural stigmas against women as well as be willing to have an open mind to see the issue and change the dynamics for our future generations.

In order to do this, parents must start by empowering their daughters without any boundaries and limitations. If this thought process becomes mainstream, we won't encounter the biases we face in everyday life. Every aspect of society that portrays women as weak, inefficient, incapable, or uneducated needs to be challenged. Those fathers who are truly concerned about raising strong daughters should be the ones advocating for them.

"Embolden Women: Unapologetically Me"

I have noticed that most students, especially girls, lack self-confidence and ownership over what they do and want. Parenting today is inherently stressful; kids have to deal with social media, peer pressure, competition, unsaid expectations, etc. Thus, it is common for kids to form opinions about what others want, and this triggers them to become harder on themselves. The ability to communicate with your children is crucial, but sharing the failures in life with them is even more essential. Your child needs to know that they can come to you to talk about all the things that didn't work out and that setbacks are completely normal.

We must teach them that they cannot be successful without a few setbacks. The key is to inspire them to keep striving forward, learn from their mistakes, and improve on their abilities. The most important thing for them is to embrace who they are "unapologetically," and be proud of it and own it. During a conversation with a friend, we discussed a Bollywood film that promoted women as eye candy.

"Embolden Women: Unapologetically Me"

As a progressive, I thought the portrayal of women was demeaning, and to my surprise, my friend, who was regarded as progressive, argued that it was just a movie - I need to lighten up. That's when it hit me how the subconscious acceptance of the incorrect portrayal of women has been greatly infiltrated by a male dominant mindset, which is construed as overreacting when challenged. Remember the normalization trap.

It is difficult to change the mindset if we subconsciously influence our growing girls to believe this trait is a woman's characteristic. Lots of things seem trivial, but if not addressed at the right time, they become deeply rooted in society. Every little thing that puts women in a place of compromise, leads to acceptance of unequal treatment, or causes women to be misused for their talents or skills, needs to be questioned at every level of society to break the centuries-old barriers that continue to exist today.

In order to celebrate women, we need to stop objectifying them and realize that their essence isn't to please men. A woman is so much more than just her body and good looks. It's time we start viewing women as intelligent, talented, successful, hardworking, and strong instead of just 'beautiful.' In my opinion, beautiful is an underrated word to describe a woman; she is so much more than just that. As with a man, a woman's looks are one component of her being, but not all of it.

We need to root for "women of substance" and not "substance women". There are several examples of women breaking glass ceilings and giving inspiration to their future generations. Women like Hedy Lamarr, Rosalind Franklin, Jeanette Rankin, and several others were the backbone of modern society. And yet, there is a disparity between the names that are whispered throughout history.

We need to find a way to enhance our presence, all the while managing a marriage, children, and our families' expectations of how we should behave and present ourselves. Even today, women are expected to carry it all, and that too, without equal opportunities, even though there is a much higher ratio of women in several leadership positions today. Leaders like Mackenzie Scott, Kamala Harris, Samia Suluhu

Hassan, and hundreds of others are still facing the same hardships as their predecessors, with only the medium of their problems changing, while the state of affairs does not.

In the early 1990s, my twin Afshan wanted to pursue a degree in fashion design; there were very few options available in India for a bachelor's degree in the fashion field. Furthermore, there were very few women in that field who were successful at that time. The most you could do is attend a private college or institute and get a diploma in that field with a 3-year associate degree program.

In those days, brands and the consumer culture of the west with big brands were not as familiar to Indians as they are now. Brands and designers were not part of the mainstream knowledge of the middle class. Mostly in regard to fashion designing, opportunities were limited, and competition to sustain was high, making it harder for many to establish it as a career. In the Indian community, in general, engineering and medicine are revered and respected, whereas liberal and fine arts education disciplines are not as celebrated and respected.

Consequently, many people in the community questioned her ability to succeed in this field. Nevertheless, my parents, being very supportive, paid for her tuition without a second thought, encouraging her to follow her passion and break barriers of the mainstream. After obtaining her diploma in three years, she joined a European company that was expanding in the Indian market as a fashion merchandiser.

Her success in securing her first job is an inspiration to many young women. After graduating from college, she saw a job posting for a fashion merchandiser with the requirement of prior experience in a newspaper. The emboldened one, despite having no previous experience, went to meet the managing director to learn more about the position. When she called him to schedule an appointment, he was impressed and intrigued by her courage and unconventional approach and agreed to meet with her. And for sure, her courage, confidence, persuasion, and determination paid off, and she got the job beyond her experience.

The rest is history. Since her first job, she has worked with a variety of big brands and is now an Executive at a very well-recognized e-Commerce company in Asia. So, by breaking the barrier, she opened a path for those who graduated after her. She was the only one among her batch of graduates to pursue a career beyond designing and led the way in merchandising.

I am so proud that she, my twin, prides herself on being "Unapologetically Me" - truly an "Emboldened" woman. We, women, face different challenges at every stage of our lives. Every culture, country, and religion have unwritten rules and expectations for what women can and cannot do. As I mentioned in the earlier chapter, most of society's rules are set by men and endorsed by women in the past, who were made to believe that these are the true values that need to be followed, no matter what their race, religion, or culture may be.

The expectations for women; to compromise on their careers for their families, be less aggressive than men at work, be paid less, or have no right to abortion even at the cost of their lives, are some examples of women being controlled by male-dominant social norms. There is no question that these unspoken expectations are at the root of all atrocities committed by both men and women against women in the name of families, traditions, culture, etc.

The conversations I have with my daughter Sarah are what gave me inspiration for this book. Although she is just 15, she is very clear about her expectations of life and especially about her "Unapologetically Me" quotient. Ever since she was a little girl, her questions and thoughts have amazed me. She is a strong advocate of girl power and women's independence.

A few years ago, when she was 8, she said, "Mom, I will only marry someone who can cook; I don't want to be the one cooking every day like you." The fact that she noticed this was mind-blowing. As parents, you must be aware of the surroundings and environment you're raising a child in because it greatly impacts their mindset. Sometimes, they can adopt the same norms/values, and other times they can teach you the things that are wrong. Moreover, when she was 11, she told me, "Mom, I am not moving to another town after marriage just because my spouse lives there. Why is it that most women leave everything behind to follow their spouse, boyfriend, or fiancé?".

"Why is it assumed that a woman's career goals are less important than a man's?" Can you imagine an 11-year-old with such conviction? Whenever she asks these questions, contemplating the reasons why things are as they are, I feel so proud and inspired. For the record, my husband did move to the city we live in for my job, and I believe that has enabled my kids to see things differently. Every action of yours has an influence on your kids' minds and molds them into that thought process to a certain extent.

Back to my daughter, she has always had a very curious mind, and I ensured not to shun her curiosity but answer her questions to the best of my ability. It brings me great joy to know I am raising a daughter who has a strong will and clear expectations for her worth. Our future generation needs strong-minded girls who have the courage to challenge the unfair and unequal treatment of women and embrace women's power without prejudice. "Freedom of expression is a fundamental human right."

This right must be available to everyone regardless of gender, race, or religion. All women must have equal access to voice their opinions and contribute to all aspects of society. You cannot shut out 50% of the voice in this world and stop half of the power from contributing to the progress and growth of society. A woman's first step to being "Emboldened" and

"Unapologetically Me" is to take a stand for herself and her wants without feeling guilty. I encourage all women readers to embrace their unique identities without feeling confined or limited.

You don't need anyone's confirmation or validation. Each of us is born with unique traits and talents, and we should embrace them without any inhibitions and containment, believing in and embracing our abilities. All women should be ambassadors and advocates for one another, willing and eager to help each other in their life journey. I believe all women should be able to support themselves, and we need to have women at all tables.

In my opinion, there is no place in this world where women cannot be or shouldn't be, and for that reason, the most important thing to do is to make sure girls have access to education; this is the ultimate key to women's empowerment. It is imperative for every woman to be able to decide for herself what she wants from life, to put herself above others, and to have a strong voice in all facets of life. We need to invest in tools and techniques that allow women to be self-confident, effective communicators, and willing to face a barrier head-on.

How can we create more opportunities for women to gain strength? Let's be the change agents, especially people like me, my sisters, my daughter, and many others who can inspire, support, and enable other girls and women to achieve success. My goal is to change the lives of women for the better. If I can inspire one to three women with this book, I feel like I am giving something back to the community and society.

Key Takeaway:

Parents are the very first people that a child interacts with and learns from. Thus, it is the responsibility of every parent to play their part in understanding and rising above the stigmas set against women. They must strive to teach their daughters how to be and live unapologetically and shape their thinking in a healthy way. It's time for parents to break those unnecessary and backward boundaries that halt their daughters from succeeding and moving in society freely. I also strongly feel that there needs to be a greater awareness of how women are portrayed in ads/movies, objectified, and given lesser roles in the entertainment industry.

For example, often, they will be shown as dumb or made to wear sexually attractive clothing. Sometimes, there are hidden messages being passed around across various platforms and industries. Moreover, instead of shunning our daughters, we must give them the space to ask questions and challenge beliefs and norms instead of repeating the same old toxic cycles.

"Embolden Women: Unapologetically Me"

Chapter 5: Girl's Education and Gender Equality

There's a reason why so much emphasis has been placed on education. Education is a powerful tool that determines and enhances every aspect of our lives. Irrespective of our career or discipline, it stays with us throughout and shapes our intellectual skills. Education helps to develop character, moral values, mindset, and personality for the rest of our lives. To sum it up, it allows us to make decisions, choose, think, challenge, reflect, analyze, respond, and, most importantly, tolerate diversity.

Now, the million-dollar question is, if we take that power away from 49.58% of our population, how will society progress? Almost 50% of the population refers to females that are deprived of education. Education enables girls and women to compete at every level of society and is as important as it is to males.

Individuals and society benefit from an educated population, which is of utmost significance to socio-economic growth.

Countries advance when their entire populace is intelligent, capable, and competent. Education provides one with the ability to assist themselves in any way they require, even stay at home mothers, for that matter. If a mother is educated, she will be able to make far better nutrition and healthcare decisions for her children. If more girls attend school, there will be a greater probability of them entering the workforce, which will enable households, communities, and countries to rise out of poverty.

Education is a catalyst for the future building of society. This gives you the opportunity to expand your mind by exposing you to a diverse group of people and ideas. This allows you to make sensible decisions and provide you the freedom to think logically. In my introduction, I told you about the discussion I had with my dad when I told him I wanted to be a voice for women when I grew up. He agreed and said you can if you have the ability and knowledge to do so. Those words emboldened me drastically because what he said was so critical, "to have ability and knowledge."

In layman's terms, my father basically implied that knowledge empowers people to make a difference, and ability gives them the power to make a difference. Therefore, education is imperative for both knowledge and ability. Without it, we can't even begin to think of changing society. After all, it's the cornerstone to progress for all, regardless of gender. Educating our girls is one of the most effective methods for breaking down the barriers to equal opportunities.

Let's reflect on ourselves using the Agile Retrospective principle I described in Chapter 3 - "Start, Stop and Continue":

1. Start a campaign to educate girls all around the world. Today, being a sponsor/mentor for numerous girls worldwide is much easier, thanks to the advancements in technology. So, it's time to make the most of the virtual world. Let's start giving girls the same fair chance for education as boys. A great method to break down the barrier would be to build local community programs to assist in mentoring and sponsoring girls worldwide, especially since we in the U.S have a better ability to provide access to schools and education.

2. We need to become ambassadors to **Stop** unfair practices against girls in our communities and contribute to the mission to educate girls. Countless girls suffer injustice of all sorts because no one is willing to take a stand for them. Remember, you can put an end to unfair practices, injustice, violence, and abuse if you raise your voice consistently and educate the girls about their rights and freedom.

3. And finally, let's **Continue** to be the voice, raising awareness to support girls' education. Don't let your girls think they can't get a high-class education because of their gender. Let them score high, achieve their dreams, and make a life for themselves, no matter what people say.

"Embolden Women: Unapologetically Me"

Here are some hard facts to consider regarding gender equality and pay. In today's day and age, it's sad that we women don't get paid what men do in all occupations. According to the U.S Department of Labor, "Women earn 82 cents for every dollar a man earns". In the United States, fewer than a quarter of women are in congress. Only 5 percent of Fortune 500 CEOs are women, and 1 in 5 women have experienced sexual assault. We can eliminate the gender pay gap by increasing the awareness of working women and girls at school, their workplaces, and in local communities.

Along with that, we can help them raise their voices to end this gender discrimination. Not only is there a gender pay gap, but also a gender disparity in career achievement. Most women have been forced and emotionally manipulated to leave the workforce to prioritize family over work. In reality, women are compelled by circumstance and environment to sacrifice their careers. There is an unsaid notion that women are willing to sacrifice a career out of willfulness.

Because of childcare needs, several women leave the workforce, which has reduced the number of women in powerful boardroom positions. Prioritizing family over career is the biggest barrier to career advancement for women. Numerous men expect their careers to take precedence over their female partners since they want them to take primary responsibility for raising children and managing the house. This expectation by men is nothing but male domination and selfish behavior, and if you think about it, you will begin to question it yourself.

Why can your husband continue to advance in his career while you have to sacrifice yours? It's high time we instill the idea of more working women who can also manage their children and house. After all, why is a sacrifice mandatory? Coming back to the previous point, a lot of women are willing to accept the responsibility that their men want them to take, and their careers get compromised. We should stop sectioning society based on gender stereotypes in regard to primary responsibilities such as child-rearing and family support and instead focus on talent and capability.

When one partner is better at their skills and talents than the other, that should be the determining factor instead of gender when pursuing career interests. Workplaces must change their models and provide more support for family needs than just thinking about the divide between men and women. The responsibility of raising / nurturing children lies with both parents, and one of them should not be punished because of it. I had my first child when I was in my mid-20s, and it was the best time of my life, both personally and professionally.

A very promising job came my way, and I became a mother for the very first time, which was the most precious and priceless moment of my life. I was very well prepared to take care of my child and my career. I was over the moon. Enthusiastic and willing to manage both aspects of my life seamlessly. Now that I reflect on it, it was a clear mind and an emboldened attitude that allowed me to be a career-oriented woman while raising our children. Fortunately, there was never any discussion between my spouse and me as to whether I would go back to work; it was always meant to be.

I personally feel that having a supportive spouse is a huge blessing. Your significant other needs to understand what your career means to you, trust you enough to be able to manage both your kids and career, and never ask you to make a choice between the two. To my surprise, I found out that my return to work was a topic of discussion in my community circle. Several women denigrated me for being heartless and uncaring; it seemed like everyone but me was concerned about sending my child to daycare.

The saddest part of all of this was that the women who thought I was neglecting my mom duties were taught this by men. It seemed as if they lacked a mind of their own. They didn't progress with time and were stuck in the same age-old patterns of thinking. During that time, several so-called friends changed their attitude towards me, trying to convince me of the importance of giving my child my full attention because, according to them, a mother can't give full attention to her child while working.

These assumptions, remarks, and changed attitude was upsetting, but I decided not to be distracted by that noise and went ahead with my planned path. It was a choice I made and a barrier I broke for myself; the ability to withdraw from a society that prevents me from being "Unapologetically Me." One of the most challenging things for a new mother is not to feel guilty about leaving her child to go to work, and dealing with this unwanted noise makes it even more difficult.

I remember to this day the first time I parted from my son and daughter to go to work. Both times, I was in tears. I had a tough day focusing on work with lots of emotions and guilt, but on the other hand, I was equally committed to my career and wouldn't be guilty of abandoning it either. My advice to new working mothers is that it is okay to feel guilty about working and caring for your child at the same time.

The best thing you can do as a mother is not to give up on your goals and ambitions when you have a child. Remember, the rest of your identity is not supposed to vanish when you become a mother. As long as you are happy and content, you will keep your child and other members of your family happy. You can't give your full attention to anything if you have to sacrifice one thing for another. So, instead of thinking of this as a sacrifice, a better way to put it would be that "I am taking career and motherhood side by side."

You will face a couple of weak moments, but do not let them overwhelm you; remain strong and keep the promises you made to yourself and to your goals. This is your "Emboldened Woman; Unapologetically Me" moment. Don't miss it; embrace it courageously and move forward. You will become more adept at balancing your career and motherhood as time goes on. This journey is going to teach you to plan your life better and be realistic. You will become more structured, and you will learn to prioritize.

At first, it isn't easy; it requires a lot of effort, as you multitask and 'multi-think' about every task at hand. We all need to share our experiences and ideas with each other in order to create a healthy environment that encourages everyone to achieve their dreams and goals and take care of their family.

It is okay to feel tired, lost, uncertain, nervous, confused, and even anxious about the whole journey. Here are some strategies to help you cope with both:

1. It is important that you and your spouse have a candid discussion about child-rearing and make sure to discuss things like sharing responsibilities and future career plans. Remember, just because you're a mother now doesn't mean you have to put your dreams, goals, or ambitions on hold.

2. Think about how you can share the burden of childcare and house chores with your partner. If you feel like you need help, then voice that thought out. Please keep in mind that asking for help doesn't mean you're incapable; it simply means you're realistic and solution oriented.

3. You can get help from grandparents without feeling guilty. I had my mother travel from India and intermittently help me out for a few months. Not to mention, leaving your child in the presence of elders is only going to make them learn and grow as individuals. There's a lot that our elders can teach our kids.

4. Make sure you take out ample time to relax, rest, and unwind. I used to have a "Me Time Day" where I would leave my son and my spouse at home every other Sunday and be gone from noon to six. It was a day to do whatever I wanted without any limitations. I would go shopping, go to a spa, catch up with friends, or just relax at a cafe reading. The point was to have my space and time for myself, which was another "Unapologetic Me" moment. Often mothers let go of themselves while they are raising a child but trust me, a few hours of leisure/relaxation away from home is necessary to recharge you.

5. Work out a flexible schedule with your employer to accommodate your childcare needs. Employers now have more flexibility with hours and remote/hybrid working options. If your employer is not being flexible, you have the opportunity to bring about that change. Challenge them, gather people who support you, and develop campaigns to raise awareness about work-life balance and family flexibility. Collect data to understand how many women with childcare needs are struggling and how this could affect their productivity. Several organizations have realized that flexibility leads to a stress-free working environment, which leads to greater productivity.

Most of the time, female workers don't ask for flexibility out of fear of looking weak and uncommitted to their careers. The status quo won't change if women don't ask; it's all about the status quo. If you take the first step, you could inspire so many others to take a stand for themselves without feeling ashamed or thinking they are asking for too much.

Key Takeaway:

There's no surprise that a lot of girls still don't have access to education. The time and era we are living in are supposedly termed as modern. Thus, it's high time that girls get access to the same superior education that boys are expected to attain. After all, education is a basic human right, and it only serves as beneficial at large. Unfortunately, the problem lies in the mentality of society. We wish to progress, but our growth is limited because we possess a closed mindset.

In fact, most men in society view women's education as a threat to themselves, their standing, and their positions. No one wants to be enlightened, challenged, or allow the other gender to rise above. Gender equality should not be a continuous fight; it should prevail without any second thoughts. Have you ever noticed why there are much fewer women in the position of CEO/manager or in big boardroom meetings? The answer is because of gender inequality, they are not given enough opportunities to prove themselves and their capabilities. They are constantly pushed into the back seat, unfairly held back with questions, suppressed, and made to feel inferior.

The harsh truth is that not only do men think less of women, but instead, they tirelessly aim to instill that same thinking into other women they can control. We need to establish the rules and learn to cherish our dreams, goals, and ambitions to the best of our ability without any guilt or pressure from anyone; then, only will we truly embolden ourselves and live a life that is unapologetically ours.

"Embolden Women: Unapologetically Me"

Chapter 6: Talent, Strength, and Sustenance

The majority of women have difficulty marketing themselves in every aspect of their lives. It's so problematic that from an early age, we are taught to give less or no credit to ourselves, and somehow, being humble is part of that. As a result, women often miss out on golden opportunities at work. Women need to embrace their strengths and own them fearlessly.

Further, I think we should stop being modest about our abilities since men certainly don't undersell themselves but rather oversell themselves. If, being a woman, you have certain high points that you want to work in your favor, highlight them; don't shy away from them. We, women, need to learn to share our goals, needs, strengths, weaknesses, and so forth in every aspect of our lives.

The best way to combat our weaknesses is to be empowered to own and leverage our strengths. Not so long ago, I coached a friend on how to do well during a job interview. Although she had the ability to do the job well, she still second-guessed if she could meet the job requirements. In fact, it was hard for her to describe what she brought to the table. Since she was too engrossed with the application requirements, she was literally underselling herself and doubting her skillset. As a result, I had to persuade her to perceive her strengths and to turn the job requirements into a positive opportunity to learn new skills and succeed in that position.

The fact is that if we want to apply for a job, we don't have to meet every qualification; we need to stop underselling ourselves by trying to meet every requirement on the job posting. Sometimes, a certain skill might not be mentioned in the requirements, but because you possess it, it can tremendously increase your value to the organization. To achieve career growth, we should seek out jobs that offer growth opportunities, which means we must build some of the qualifications from the new job.

What matters is your talent, not your skill set. Show your potential employer your strengths through your prior achievements, which highlight how you excel at new challenges. While you're at it, let your interest and ability to learn and grow be evident to the employer. This will make you appear to be the best candidate for the job. For a lot of women, pre-interview jitters are one of the main reasons they do not get the job. Qualifications aside, there must be something in your life that you do to build confidence.

It could be rehearsing your introduction for 5 minutes every day or even just prepping for your interview with a friend. Having a person judge how you come off in an interview can help you acquire pointers to improve your first impression. But the root of the problem is still the fact that many women today simply lack the self-confidence necessary to show themselves as career-oriented women.

And the ones that do, tend to wander from the core principles of staying true to themselves. By simply rehearsing in front of a friend or a mirror, you can understand and then improve yourself in many ways. One thing I've realized in all my years is that employers are not only concerned about what a piece of paper says. Instead, they want to see how confident you are in real life, how well you sell yourself, and how efficiently you're able to apply your knowledge and talent to suit their unique business model.

Growth comes when you learn from everything and everyone all of the time, as described in the first chapter on the Emotional Intelligence Quotient. Today, women need to recognize their strengths and own them without hesitation, and to achieve that, they must train themselves to be unapologetically bold. We need the development of training programs that instill self-efficacy and sheer confidence in our future generation of women. We must enable women to recognize their abilities and capitalize on them.

We need to create a society where all women can be self-sufficient. In my opinion, women are truly empowered when they are able to be self-sufficient & self-reliant, which is when they are truly emboldened and empowered. When you're heavily dependent on someone for everything, it gives them the advantage of controlling you and your life. At times they may even make you feel like they own you, your decisions, and your actions. You may not feel it initially, but over time, you are bound to feel trapped and will eventually suffocate.

Thus, we must take away that advantage from others. Having financial independence and the ability to own your life is something every woman should strive for. Not depending on anyone else but yourself for your needs is a feeling that I want every single woman on the face of this earth to experience. We will definitely be able to do that if we are educated and understand our rights. Self-reliance and self-sustenance can be powerful vehicles for helping women "empower themselves" and be "unapologetically themselves" in every aspect of our lives. So, instead of giving up the steering wheel of your life, regain your power and decide every little and big thing by yourself. Know with certainty that you are capable enough to acquire supreme education, be self-reliant, & have no regrets about the decisions you make.

It is crucial to instill self-efficacy in girls from an early age. I mention self-efficacy so often that you must wonder what it is. An individual's self-efficacy refers to the ability to control situations, enabling them to make better choices and face challenges with confidence. Self-efficacy allows us to face problems head-on and overcome obstacles with confidence. This allows us to pursue our goals with zeal and purpose. Growing up, my mother always encouraged me to do my level best without settling for anything less.

Thanks to her, it has enabled me to continue to drive myself and be the best I can be. Similarly, if every mother encourages her daughter to do the same, it will soon add up. Self-efficacy is having a passion for your goals, which gives you the ability to chart the unknown even when it's uneasy, knowing that you are in full control. I believe that having a little bit of unease about something, whether it's a job, a project, or a hobby, gives you the motivation to do better. Good things never come out of comfort zones.

So, get uneasy and gather the inspiration and motivation to do better in all areas. Did you ever wonder why a lot of girls have low confidence and boys are often overconfident? It simply has to do with the environment, safety, culture, religion, and social norms that restrict girls during their early years. Not to mention, girls are taught to be prim and proper, and expectations for them to be a certain way are far greater as compared to boys. Usually, by the time they are old and realize how unfair things have been, it is too late for them to have the will to break that barrier.

But bear in mind that motivation and inspiration are key to discovering the inner strength that prevents them from being who they really are. We need to find ways to empower every woman to embrace her strengths and values; to cherish her femininity. In high schools, why are boys given more opportunities than girls? For example, high school football is a big deal, with funding and support from parents and schools, which allows boys to be recruited by big ten schools.

The question then becomes, what is the equal counterpart of that beyond girls reaching for the top ten schools with their individual abilities? I think most of our gender-related beliefs are set by the society in which we live. When I was a child growing up in the early 80s, the Prime Minister of India was a woman. Honestly, I never even noticed that she broke the glass ceiling; it felt very normal to me. In fact, I felt as if women were empowered in this way all over the world. Ideally, if that were the case, things would be amazing for women in every aspect of their life.

When I was eight years old, I was naive to believe that if a woman had the ability and willingness to lead, she could be a prime minister or president of a country. But that was not the case. As an eight-year-old, I was unaware of the glass ceiling and men's dominance because the most powerful person in the country then was a woman; how could an 8-year-old think women are limited? I find it sad that 50% of the population of the U.S refuses to accept the concept of a female president in this day and age. Isn't it heartbreaking to know the world's largest country has not been able to change people's mindset on how women can lead?

Hopefully, we will get there someday soon, now that we have a female vice president. Perhaps, she can pave the way for many others to come forth. Women have always been viewed as the lesser gender regardless of how educated, competent, or skilled they may be. I believe that all women should be able to sustain themselves, when necessary, as sustenance is a key part of our lives.

Moreover, all women should be educated regardless of whether they plan to pursue a career or not since it is the critical foundation for the development of society, as I mentioned in chapter five. Empowered women need not be career-oriented or even employed; a homemaker can also be empowered, so long as she chooses to be. The empowerment of women is not about forcing them to work but rather about respecting their choices.

Being a housewife has its own challenges. Despite working 24/7 without a break, they are rarely acknowledged for the sacrifices they make and how much they do for their families. In fact, they are often taken for granted by their spouses. Homemakers should build their value propositions with their families, have equal access and rights to financial support, and be able to make their own decisions without any interference.

In that partnership, one spouse is primarily responsible for raising children, and the other is supporting the family. Therefore, you have the same right to financial decisions as your spouse. In addition to recognizing the value of your hard work, your family should also acknowledge it and tirelessly appreciate you for it. You should be aware of how you deserve their gratitude and appreciation to keep going even when things get tough. Lastly, you must be capable and willing to be self-sufficient in the hour of need, and for that, you need to have familiarity with different skills, even if you are not employed.

Another misconception I want to debunk is that quite a few women feel they are not 'skilled' because they are unemployed. This is a completely wrong mindset and approach to things. In fact, if you think along these lines, you are creating a huge barrier for yourself. Even if you are a homemaker, the way you manage the key responsibilities of a home and raise your children is a skill and art itself. Your skills are a potential asset to be used at the right time.

Apart from that, when you have the opportunity to sharpen your skills, I recommend that you attend a community college, vocational training, self-development workshop, or learn other skills that best suit your interests. Sustenance is the primary need of mankind and should not be determined by or restricted to gender. As a woman, you must know how to sustain yourself when the need arises because life is unpredictable. Unexpected things may happen, and when they do, you must be prepared. Women empowerment comes from the courage to handle any situation and the ability to deal with the entity known as life. My mother is one of my greatest role models for empowering women.

During my primary school years, my mom happily volunteered to teach sewing to the less fortunate and poor. Although she was a homemaker raising five children and had no help around the house, she still found time to help others in the community. Where there is a will, there is a way. Her intention was to provide women from low-income neighborhoods with the opportunity to learn to sew and develop the skills to work in a garment factory. Upon not being able to get a space, she decided to start free classes at her home. My mother didn't want anything in return from them.

As a child, I was not happy to see a bunch of women sitting around in my living room with stacks of material and paper, and I remember asking my mother why this was necessary. She told me that these women could feed their families if they were self-sufficient. After completing the coursework, one of the women came home and spoke about how she had now enrolled in a garment factory and gave lots of blessings to my mom while tearing up. She shared how she managed to feed and send her children to school.

I was proud of my mom then, but now I realize she had a significant impact on the upcoming generation of women who were able to send their children to school. Without skills, those women and their families would have continued to live in poverty with no means of feeding and educating their children. Furthermore, they would also be dependent on others for financial support, and their life would be controlled and dominated by those offering assistance. Over a decade, my mom taught at least 300 women.

Imagine if even 50% of those families had children who are now working in professional fields or vocational jobs; that would truly enable a progressive society, and my mom accomplished that. No idea is too small. If you have a creative and effective way to help someone, don't wait around. You may think you're changing the life of one person, but that's just the surface. Every one person's life you change: you're changing the lives of so many others simultaneously.

My mother's life is a great example of how you don't have to be a working woman to make a difference. You just have to make use of good opportunities for yourself and other women around you. There is no set rule to making a difference; it's all about how you want to take on a challenge. My mother empowered other women by allowing them to be independent and care for their families. Regardless of what we do and how we live, we can all help to build a better future for other women.

You don't have to do something big to enable others; start small but start somewhere. There are many women role models and heroes in and around us. All we need to do is tap into that part of ourselves. We can all inspire and empower one another. Inspiration does not necessarily come from public figures, nor does it come only from famous people.

Often, inspiration and learning come from those closest to us. There are many ways we can contribute and help elevate other women. Take a moment to think of the women in your life: your mom, sister, mother-in-law, best friend, coworker, etc., and how they may have influenced or inspired you at different stages of your life. You will realize how each of them may have had a huge impact on who you are today.

Key Takeaway:

I believe that talent goes a long way. In the end, we as women should be confident in what we have to offer instead of doubting ourselves or seeking validation from others. It's time to raise the bar high and not expect anything less than what we deserve, be it in the house, at your job, amongst your social circle, and so forth. Always keep in mind that there is beauty in your strength and struggle, and the world needs to see more of that.

Being able to sustain yourself is a life skill I swear by. When you rely on nobody else but yourself, you will realize your true power and control in life. You are the master of your destiny, so don't shy away from taking things into your own hands. Lastly, when you are able to help another woman, do so fearlessly and positively because, for every one woman you help, you will be helping a whole race.

"Embolden Women: Unapologetically Me"

Chapter 7: Never Underestimate Your Power to be You

As the title suggests, this chapter is going to be focused on not underestimating yourself and being yourself fearlessly. I believe every now and then, we are told to be a certain way, follow through with the set expectations and be anything but ourselves. Since we are constantly hearing the same thing from different people, it gets reinforced, and we may even start to act on it. You see, that is the main problem.

At the end of the day, you have to learn to block out all that unnecessary noise; be bold, be strong and be who you are! There will be times in your life when people will knock you down, laugh at you, question your abilities/talents and make you feel unworthy. It's always easier said than done, but in such situations, it's essential that you do not underestimate your abilities or lose self-confidence. When you face these circumstances, breathe and think logically instead of instantly feeling inferior.

When you think rationally, you'll be able to recognize that what is being said or assumed about you has nothing to do with you or your talents. Instead, it largely has everything to do with the other person and what's going on in their shallow mind. So just casually shrug it off and continue to be your best self. Boldness and confidence require accepting yourself without apologies or feeling obligated to justify yourself.

We need to stop interpreting our perception of ourselves through the perspective of others if we actually want to learn to shape it. There's no denying that we all want to please others, whether they are our parents, friends, teachers, colleagues, or bosses. We are taught to satisfy others as a result of our upbringing and background. As we grow older, we begin to realize that we are often faced with things that make us uncomfortable, unhappy, and dissatisfied.

But we continue to do so out of fear of rejection. The truth is we crave acceptance no matter how much we try to deny it. It takes massive courage and confidence to be yourself and own who you are. When you accept what others think about you, you are giving others the power and freedom to define you. If you want to be YOU, you must take back your power from others to define your identity. My personal belief is that the common problem of wanting to be liked or accepted stems from a lack of confidence.

When you are completely confident about yourself, your abilities, and your skills, you don't need to seek validation or acceptance from others. As a result, no one will have the chance to define you but yourself. When you are so certain of who you are and own every little aspect of your being, you keep all the power to yourself instead of handing it over to someone else. At that moment, you realize that you are in control. Unfortunately, women have a terrible habit of underestimating and underselling themselves.

Quite often, we fail to realize what we are capable of. Trust me; if you were able to tap into just a tad bit of your true potential, you would be amazed at the things you can accomplish.

Realize Your True Potential

The question I want to ask you today is, have you ever stopped and thought, 'what is something a woman can't do?' If you begin making a list, I'm sure you will have unlimited pages to fill. I want you to count them and feel good about yourself so let's name a few:

- Being able to provide education and all sorts of learning
- Being able to secure good jobs and have successful careers
- Being able to raise and nurture kids
- Being able to manage the house and have a career simultaneously
- Being able to multitask
- Being able to effectively manage money and save
- Being able to participate in and play sports
- Being able to lead and acquire leadership positions
- Being able to reproduce

Although the above-mentioned list is not very elaborate when you start listing the things, I'm sure each page will remind you of how amazing you are, and you will go straight to cloud nine, bursting with joy. Mind you, I'm not only talking about highlighting the big things you have done as a woman, but each and every little thing counts too. The things we feel are insignificant actually hold a lot of value. We just fail to recognize them.

I don't completely blame you for not being able to see the value you have, but I hope to instill the realization and firm belief that you are enough and are doing a wonderful job in life. Another thing that I can swear by is taking the time out to appreciate yourself for what you are doing and how far you have come from a little girl to a mature woman.

Tolerance refers to the ability to accept and respect other viewpoints without imposing one's own beliefs on others. The reason why I bring up tolerance is because only tolerant people can truly be themselves. If you know how to respect yourself, you learn to respect others around you. When you have the power to be you, you are able to openly and unapologetically communicate your views and take full ownership of your identity for the way you think, behave and look.

Ownership is another thing that we women need to work on improving because it will most certainly do wonders and take us far ahead in life. The point to be noted here is that taking ownership should not be considered wrong. If males can take ownership in different ways in both their professional and personal lives, why can't women?

Always remember there is no need for you to seek approval and permission from others if you really treasure yourself. What matters the most is how you see yourself in the mirror. Whenever you feel pressured, empower yourself to define and own yourself; once you do so, you have nothing to fear. You will seamlessly be able to overcome rejection by giving yourself the priority and permission to be "YOU." Do not hold back due to a fear of rejection or failure, and never underestimate the power of being yourself and taking ownership of it.

I'm sure this will give you a whole new perspective on life and allow you to make better decisions and make healthier choices for yourself. Recently, at one of my hair appointments, my hairstylist Taylor shared with me that she encourages women to follow their hearts with how they want to look. In her view, hairstyle and color can be a direct expression of your identity. Thus, there is no need to apologize or feel conscious of how you choose to wear it.

Let's be honest; does this remind you of how many times you wanted to dye your hair a funky color because that speaks to you, but you didn't end up going for it out of the fear of rejection? Well, this is your big sign to get that uncommon hair dye, rock the color you love, and flaunt it unapologetically. Remember, you don't have to live to please others. The very first person you should please is yourself.

You need to be happy with your choices and live life on your own terms. According to Taylor, how you style your hair can make a statement about you. She advises women to follow their hearts and minds rather than worrying about what their significant others, friends, or family think. Not to mention, she practices what she preaches and experiments with her own hair without seeking recognition from others. If she's content with dying her hair half purple and half blue, she goes for it. She never spends a split-second contemplating about what people say or think.

As a matter of fact, I can see that she's very secure as a person. Taylor is truly an 'Emboldened Woman' who is unapologetic about herself and encourages others to do the same. Her aim is to elevate women to feel better physically, mentally, and emotionally after each session with her. This conversation touched me to the core. My admiration for her lies in her dedication to empowering women. Her mindset is in check, and she never misses an opportunity to positively change the flawed perceptions, so many women carry. Therefore, I am even more convinced that each woman can play a key role in empowering the other, and you can do that without underestimating the power of being 'you.'

Remember, "Never underestimate your power to be YOU'" because it's not easy, and it takes a lot to be YOU! I firmly believe that just one person can make a change and can also start the chain of fostering a change. I want to challenge all my readers to dream and think big. If your dreams don't scare you, they are not big enough. We need to ask ourselves if we are living our life unapologetically according to our own terms or if we are living like slaves according to the terms set by others in the name of culture, tradition, and norms.

It's time to ponder over if we have the freedom to choose and live our lives as we wish. This question has no right or wrong answer. What is right for one person may not necessarily be right for another. What matters is your happiness. Don't let yourself feel lost, confused, or trapped, due to others' perceptions and expectations. Its time you break free of those chains.

Maintain Balance

We all face countless hurdles and challenges as working women because of previously established norms, culture, beliefs, and so forth. All of us must find the correct work-life balance and learn to deal with challenges, especially women from eastern cultures. Having too many boundaries and expectations puts women in a disadvantaged position.

While it's easy to cry and complain, let's change the narrative. Let's create situations that are bound to be advantageous for us and ensure we are victorious. We need to learn to stand our ground without feeling guilty and challenge the traditional norms. This is a battle that no one else will fight for us. There is no need to accept limitations set by others as long as we know what we are doing and how things are aligning. I'm sure you must have heard the saying that a happy woman means a happy family.

While the man may be considered to be the head of the family, the woman is the foundation of the entire house. It's her job to ensure the right balance, and that can only be done when she is happy on the inside. How can we inspire our children if we don't take a stance on our aspirations and goals? Our children are constantly learning from us and looking up to us. It is likely that they will follow and preach what they see regularly.

So, we must show them the good, the happy, and the positive side of things. We must instill the right education and values in them from a tender age. The question is, if we can't do it ourselves, how can anyone else do it for us? To live life on one's own terms, without limitations, is what it means to be 'Unapologetically Me.' Let's not wait around for others to give us permission to live, enjoy life freely, and chase our dreams.

Key Takeaway:

As tough as it is to hear, there's no denying that you have lived enough years of your life trying to fit in, please others, confine yourself to the set expectations, and seek acceptance/validation from others. In the process of doing so, you have lost your voice, perception, confidence, beauty, power, and most of all, your identity to be who you wish to be, unapologetically. But this is not the end; think of it as the beginning. The fact that you picked up this book speaks volumes. I know you can shine and allow others to get out of the darkness. There is always a light at the end of a dark and gloomy tunnel; you just have to be brave enough to switch it on.

"Embolden Women: Unapologetically Me"

Chapter 8: There is No Winning

Women have continued to suffer for centuries, and it's a tale as old as time. Sometimes, we feel as if we have conquered the world and made good progress, and the very next moment, we realize we are far from conquest. The reality is that we are far from truly being empowered. As a matter of fact, even the smallest victories and achievements make us feel superior, and that is exactly where the problem lies. My question is, why have we set the bar so low?

Society and, most importantly, more than half of the men in society have conditioned and programmed our minds in a way that we easily feel amused by minor achievements. Therefore, we lose sight of the bigger picture. If women want to win in the right manner, an important milestone to achieve is learning to set the bar higher. In all my years, I've realized that men are trained to set the bar high. They have high expectations, high standards, and high requirements for themselves, which they are not willing to compromise or settle on.

But this very same ideology for women is a foreign concept. Women with high standards, & requirements are called bossy, uptight, know-it-alls, etc. As if you are being punished for having opinions or a sense of authority. An assertive woman is considered bossy, but a man who is assertive is considered a leader. A woman who expresses her intelligence is a 'know-it-all,' but a man doing the very same is intelligent.

A woman who emphasizes on processes and rules is 'uptight,' but a man who does the same has a sense of ownership. The idea that I want to instill in each of you is that there is no room for dejection, we need to empower ourselves to believe in our abilities, there is no stopping, and we need to keep marching forward irrespective of challenges we face be it at work, school, or home front. We need to carry the baton first for ourselves, and then for other women.

We can't get disheartened, and neither can we stop trying. Remember, the minute you feel disheartened, your mindset, energy, and focus will weaken, and you will doubt your own abilities. Doubt and fear will creep into your mind and hover over you like a stormy cloud. Although staying positive in difficult situations is tough and can take a toll on your mental and emotional health, it is something that we must actively strive for. I have said this before, and I will say it again.

Women are made of steel, and if we tap into our strength, we will be unstoppable. All women must champion their own empowerment. Additionally, they must also make men around them, be it at home, work, or social places, think about the critical need for fair/equal chances for women in all walks of life. Let's make sure we are not casually taken for granted or perceived as lesser beings. I encourage you to find your strength and break free from all the weak links that have become a part of you.

Trust me, you are strong enough to survive in this world and make your mark on it too. A lot of women are stuck with the idea of what would happen if they tried, and it doesn't work out. But let me tell you this; even if you try to achieve something and it doesn't work out, you still win. You had the guts to head straight into something that frightened and intimidated you. That in your eyes should be counted as bravery, and this perspective will take you very far.

If you remember Chapter 3, failure is the key to success; you need to learn to fail fast and find alternative solutions. We can't not fail, and it's okay to fail, provided we find a corrective action/solution to it; It's a part of learning and growing. We need to cherish that! Women are deprived of various things due to race, religion, and culture. There is too much of a fuss between what to do and what not to do. There are too many taboos that are meant to confuse and discourage women. We need to break those barriers; we need to raise the bar and standards set by others for us.

It's time we build our own expectations, requirements, and ideologies. It's time we stop accepting defeat. Instead, we must courageously look at it and challenge it with all our might. A tried and tested technique that I can swear by is being willing to accept a challenge. When you program your mind up for a challenge, you're more motivated and driven to get a positive outcome. Thus, you invest more time and energy in preparing and setting yourself up for victory.

This brings me to discuss the retirement message in Vogue magazine from Serena Williams, who is a prominent name in the tennis world. Serena has successfully been ranked as the #1 Singles Player by the Women's Tennis Association. Moreover, she has also efficiently bagged twenty-three Grand-Slam Single titles, which are, to date, the most achieved by any player in the Open Era. While her list of achievements and victories is an elaborate one, the point I want to make with her reference is bigger than the number of trophies she has won. Serena Williams' retirement message in

Vogue magazine, in my opinion, is nothing short of an inspiration, the epitome of strength and courage, as well as an unapologetic, fearless statement on who she is and what drove her.

The raw, vulnerable, and emotional things she says in her retirement message should serve as an eye-opener for all the women in the world. After all, I believe there is beauty in owning up to everything you have done and how you have fought to be on the top and kept pushing even when the light begins to fade. Undoubtedly, in my mind, Serena has been exemplary in showing how to excel at something, make a living out of it, to not hear no for an answer, and for not stopping until the goal is a reality.

Talking about rights, I would like to shed light on two popular and powerful Hollywood celebrities you all may be aware of. One is not only an American stand-up comedian, actor, and author. He is much more than what meets the eye. Although he made his name in the entertainment industry and stood tall in the limelight, his dark side shined equally bright. He has been the subject of highly publicized sexual assault accusations by several women.

Not to mention, he was also accused of raping approximately sixty women, committing drug-facilitated assault, sexual abuse of children, and sexual misconduct. Unsurprisingly, he has tried to maintain his image and innocence, but the truth can't be hidden for too long. Despite the fact that he faced the music, his career was affected, and his reputation went down the drain; he was able to escape. In 2018, he was convicted of the wrongs he committed and sentenced to a three to ten year-long prison sentence.

However, in 2021, unfortunately, his conviction was overturned by the Pennsylvania Supreme Court. If the injustice isn't evident in this particular case, let's take a look at another example. He, who is an American actor and producer by profession, has also played a negative part in carrying out a sick agenda toward women. In fact, the disturbing similarities between both would make them seem as though they were cut from the same cloth. The reason is both are predators, and the only difference between them is their preference and mode of preying on the victim.

The main reason why I'm highlighting these men is to substantiate the argument of how there are many others like them who play a significant part in oppressing women and go unpunished simply because most of the women don't speak up out of fear. We need to contemplate this, where are we failing as a society? How do we enable little boys to grow up into more responsible individuals willing to respect women?

How can we teach our girls how not to let anyone, under any circumstance, violate them physically or mentally? How can we instill courage in our girls and give them the confidence to stand up for themselves? Look around the world, from Afghanistan to India, to even the U.S.A, women's rights are violated every day. They are told what to wear, how to behave, and when to abort.

"Embolden Women: Unapologetically Me"

Each time in the name of political and religious doctrines serving the society. Why is it that all their roads to betterment begin with the violation of women's rights and freedom? We need to build female champions in schools, colleges, at work, and on the home front. Every little violation must be questioned; none should be overlooked. I remember while growing up in India, I was once visiting a friend and encountered that, in her house, women of the family ate after the men. They were not allowed to sit and eat at the table together with the male members of their family.

Also, the male members of the family got the better portion of the meal, with women left to manage with the leftovers. I felt awkward and uncomfortable, but that scene never left my mind. I didn't want to offend or impose on my friend, so I let it be and never questioned her then. It always perplexed me as to how educated women easily accept such things in the name of culture and religion. Now, almost 35 years later, I still see that concept in Indian TV shows trying to portray women doing that to be noble and fully committed to their families. I wonder how a nation can progress if the majority of its media, in the name of entertainment, portrays women in a subdued and weak manner.

I sometimes wonder if we are any better off or worse than the women 200 years ago. What true progress have we made if we still need to hold back from communicating openly? We try to fit in a box for how we dress and look and while we still seek affirmation from male counterparts in all aspects of our lives. I do not want to make you feel dejected or low, but I certainly want to raise a sense of urgency for change in how we behave and what we settle for; it's time to wake up and smell the coffee.

We cannot go on like this anymore; I urge all my readers to respect their own identity, value their unique skills, don't let others tell you where to draw the boundaries. It is up to you to claim your power over your life and own it, and if you do, you will rock at it!

Key Takeaway:

Women must up their game and can't settle for less; we need to seek out ways to get above and beyond the set stereotypical roles and responsibilities. There is no harm in trying; it's better to fail while trying than to not do anything. We know it feels like there is no winning, but we can't stop now; we need to keep marching forward. If not now, when?

"Embolden Women: Unapologetically Me"

Chapter 9: How Can You Turn Failures into Opportunities

Failure is part and parcel of life; although we don't like to acknowledge it, it's a fundamental element of success. Our first instinct to failure is to feel ashamed because of how humiliating failure makes us feel. But it's never too late to shift our perspective. A lot of times, the way we perceive failure is problematic. Instead of thinking of failures as the end of everything, we need to optimize failure as a path to learning.

The key is to learn from our failures and move on. There is no point brooding over it, holding on to it, and letting opportunities slip by, just feeling dejected and playing victim to it. I, for one, want all women to break free of this troublesome ideology, pick themselves up, and start all over again. I want you to recognize that failure does not mean you can't accomplish what you set your mind to.

In fact, failure is just a steppingstone on the road to success. The way I see it, if you don't fail, how will you learn and grow as an individual? Remember, it's all about perception, and your mind needs to be fed with positive thoughts to have a constructive approach to things. It's highly essential that we don't let setbacks tear us down because failure is full of great opportunities for growth. I agree that failure is a very strong and disheartening word. It sits on the other end of a scale with success which is why learning how to overcome failure counts.

My take on this is instead of viewing success and failure as a seesaw of opposites, think of them as complements as they can flow toward and away from one another. The flow may contain opportunities to minimize failure and optimize success. Neither stays constant in our lives. Both success and failure are dynamic. They shift according to your situation, environment, and the people in your life. Remember agile methodology in Chapter 3: where I discuss it's okay to fail if you recognize it with corrective action and move on. Life is not much different, in-fact that is the whole point, no one is perfect, and we can't always make decisions/choices that yield the results we want.

We just need to be smart in recognizing it sooner than later and change course for the better. Many times, when men fail, they continue to try and find alternatives to move on, and for the most part, the women in their lives don't undermine their abilities or question their judgment to do it right the next time; they become their support system. But in the same scenario, when a woman fails, stereotypical viewpoints both from men and women embark on their holistic being of why they failed.

They are constantly judged for what they didn't do well and where they went wrong without giving them a second chance. The sad part is we women let them do that to us, by giving them the power to tell us what our capabilities and limits are. We have somehow been taught for generations to be controlled by other mindsets.

Most of the time, we even fail because we stop trying or are trying something based on the ideology or conception of others, mostly men in our life and around us. I strongly think the mindset for generations about role-play of man and woman makes it harder for women to not see their failures in the eyes of others. And not only do they fail because they are roleplaying, but they are not willing to try beyond a certain point, accepting limits set by others on how hard they should try. We need to first recognize irrespective of gender, we all fail, and there is no one good or bad reason.

We just need to acknowledge and seek out new opportunities. We need to believe in ourselves and our abilities; we have the skill of attaining what we desire, breaking boundaries, and putting ourselves in a position of success. We must have the conviction that we can do it, and we are not going to settle for less than what we deserve, even if it means failing multiple times, learning from it, and keep on going. We need to first agree that what we consider as failure is truly a failure, and second, that we are proud we tried and failed instead of not trying at all. Failure is for the courageous; you can't stop trying due to the fear of failure.

See below a special exercise you could try to turn failures into opportunities. In order to identify opportunities for converting failure to success, start by recalling a specific situation in which you failed. You don't necessarily need to jot down your thoughts on paper in a journal; that can be done on your phone, too, making it easy to analyze on the go.

The following is a list of questions that I have sorted out, and you can add yours too:

1. Were my expectations logical and reasonable?

2. Was my motivation in place, or was it a reflection of someone else's interests?

3. Did I have the important tools or resources?

4. Did I put in the required amount of effort?

5. What were the circumstances out of my control or influence?

6. Did I correctly position myself to get the opportunity I longed for?

7. How much of my focus/judgment was affected by external factors?

8. Did I have the right intention to begin with?

9. What are some of the things that I could do differently?

10. Was my mental and emotional state fit to grasp the opportunity?

11. What were some of the key things that I lacked and could have resulted in my failure?

After you have made a list and gone through the questions, the next step is to identify what you've learned from your failure. Soon, you will have at least one important lesson, if not more, to apply in the future. One potential route to success may involve being prepared to try again with improved savvy, higher self-awareness, less anxiety or fear, and more determination. But that's not all; there's a lot more to it.

In my opinion, numerous things in life require planned action, proper thinking, and a strategy. But above all, it requires you to have complete control of the decision in your own hand and the courage to own it without any fear and inhibition.

Here are some powerful ways that you can follow and make goal attainment simpler.

Tools/Ways to turn every failure into an opportunity:

1. Learn to accept your mistakes and acknowledge the fact that things didn't go as planned. It's imperative to acknowledge what went wrong instead of obsessing about fixing something that is not working. We, women, tend to do that a lot; we set the bar so high for ourselves that we then get into the quagmire of wanting to fix it. At times there is no fixing; we just need to move on. Acceptance might hurt your ego at first. However, when you practice it often, you will learn, change, and grow as a person. Not to mention, the ego factor will be swept under the rug.

153

2. While making mistakes is not a problem, not taking the opportunity to learn from them is a definite mistake. The point to be noted is that there is a potential for growth in every mistake. So, get rid of the fear or shame of making mistakes. It's about time you care less about what others think and alter your mindset. How will you learn, unlearn, and relearn if you don't make mistakes?

3. We must be extra careful with how we speak to ourselves. Despite the fact that many ignore this factor, negative self-talk can be incredibly damaging, especially in the case of failure. Thus, we must be mindful of how we talk to ourselves and not say anything that makes us feel worthless. I'm not implying that you shouldn't allow yourself to feel what you do after a setback. Instead, let it sting but stay optimistic, indulge in healthy affirmations, and get back on track. And, for sure, don't seek affirmation from others, it's your battle to fight, and you are fully capable of fighting it.

4. Don't let your failures define you or your worth. It's essential to remember that your future can still be far better than you envisioned it. My advice is to talk about what happened but stay focused on what lies ahead and be willing to embrace the good. Again, not based on others' definition of good but on your own.

5. Consistency is the key. Be consistent and watch how beautifully the universe aligns things for you. Remember, what you do daily counts more than what you occasionally do. Strength doesn't come from the things you can easily do; it comes from mastering the things you thought you could never do. Learn to dust yourself off, get up with dignity and move on, unbothered by the past. What you do in your present should be done consistently.

7. You don't have to go through a failure all alone, and there is no shame in asking for help. We are afraid to reach out for assistance because we fear being judged or thought of as incapable and incompetent. At times, failure will keep you stuck in your old ways. Don't make things difficult for yourself. Talk to close family and friends and find a coach/ mentor who can support you and has the relevant expertise to guide you toward success.

8. There's no denying that honesty is the best policy, and when it comes to transforming failures into opportunities, honesty holds a lot of weight. One of the most crucial parts of dealing with failures involves pondering over what happened. We must be completely honest with ourselves. While it's easy to distract ourselves, facing the truth requires more work, but if we don't confront it, we don't learn from it. And if you don't learn, you're setting yourself up for failure all over again. I would like to quote how Albert Einstein said we should not do the same thing over and again and expect a different outcome. Therefore, if we don't derive a lesson from our failures, then we are doomed to repeat them.

9. Focus on taking time out to nurture and improve yourself. Failure doesn't discriminate; everyone experiences that at some point. The trick lies in learning to deal with it and making a difference. A few common reasons why failures make room in our life is due to lack of preparation, ill-planning, fear, or bad luck. Know with certainty that every problem has a solution, so start working on your problem areas one by one. You must do everything in your power and capacity to improve, resolve, rectify and develop. And remember, you are your own competition, don't compare yourself to others to determine your success, and don't let others drive it for you either.

10. Purge out the negativity; this is another helpful way I swear by. I believe it's essential that we flush those negative thoughts and confide in people we trust in the process. Negativity will hold you back more than anything in life and make you feel stuck. As I mentioned earlier in Chapter 1: don't be toxic even in the worst of situations; always be optimistic. Like I tell my kids past is gone, and we have no control over the future; the only thing that we have in our control is the present, which we can own and make the most out of it.

Key Takeaway:

Failures are inevitable, and one thing that I

want all women out there to understand is failing is not as bad as you think it to be. As I mentioned above, it's all about perspective, and that's what you need to work on. However, this chapter touches on some powerful tips that you can use. The main thing is about applying and practicing the techniques mentioned above.

It is imperative that we change the perception that most women are weak, fearful, and incompetent. One way of doing that is by being skilled enough to turn our failures into opportunities and maximize them. We must train our minds and hearts to see the good in every situation, learn to be headstrong, and ever so determined to take what's ours. If men have the skill of attaining whatever they desire, breaking boundaries, and putting themselves in a position for success, why can't we do the same?

I want you to reflect on who is stopping you. When you think long and hard, you'll realize the only person stopping you is the one standing in front of you in the mirror. We must learn to transform ourselves and change the rules of the game. We must think highly of ourselves; we can't be defined by our failures; we can't limit our progress. We are destined for greatness! After all, it's now or never!

"Embolden Women: Unapologetically Me"

160

Chapter 10: My Body My Right – Roe V. Wade

As previously mentioned by me in Chapter 2, fighting a mindset is harder than fighting an individual mind. Women have tried to raise their voices against things they don't agree with, but for the most part, their voices are curtailed, not giving them the desired recognition. I cannot complete this book without providing some details and context to Roe V. Wade. For those of you who may not be aware of the topic or debate in question, Roe V. Wade was a landmark legal decision that was issued on 22nd January 1973 in the United States because of a particular case.

An unmarried woman named McCorvey, who later became known as Jane Roe, had filed a case because she wanted to legally and safely end her pregnancy. Fortunately, the court understood her perspective on abortion and ruled in her favor by striking down the Texas law. For the first time, the court recognized the constitutional right to privacy and thought it was broad enough to encompass a woman's decision to keep or terminate her pregnancy.

As a result, the procedure was effectively legalized across the United States of America. Undoubtedly, this was a great achievement for Jane Roe and all the other women. Roe successfully rendered all previous laws unconstitutional and made abortion services safer and far more accessible to women throughout the country.

Moreover, the court's decision also set a legal precedent that affected more than about thirty subsequent Supreme Court cases that involved restrictions on access to abortion. Before Roe V. Wade, abortion was known to be illegal throughout most of the country since the 19th century. Not to mention, from the 1973 ruling, several states started imposing restrictions on abortion rights, and the light began to fade. Unfortunately, what seemed to be a hope, victory, and much-needed right for countless women was soon overturned by the Supreme Court. Roe V. Wade was overturned on 24th June 2022.

It was stated that there was no longer a federal constitutional right to have an abortion despite the fact that the demand for abortions was evident in the data. Nearly 930,000 legal abortions were recorded in 2020, while there were 862,000 in 2017, which is simply an indication of the increasing need for safe, affordable, legal, and respectful abortion care.

Abortion before Roe V. Wade:

As I mentioned previously, abortion was previously illegal. A few of the early regulations regarding abortion were enacted in the 1820s and 1930s. There were careful dealings with the sale of highly injurious drugs that women used to induce abortions. Even though the drugs were dangerous and, in fact, fatal to women, their advertisement and sale continued. In my opinion, this speaks volumes if you listen to the message behind it.

During the late 1850s, an American Medical Association called for abortion to be criminalized. Some argue that this was partly done to eliminate the competitors of doctors, who were none other than homeopaths and midwives. On the other hand, some nativists were alarmed since the growing population of the country was mainly anti-abortion immigrants. Thus, they feared a declining birth rate. Throughout the 18th century, there were multiple bans on abortion at any stage of pregnancy. In the year 1965, the U.S Supreme Court also banned the distribution of birth control to married couples.

In 1972, the Supreme Court struck down a law that prohibited the distribution of contraceptives to unmarried couples. Fast forward, 1970 was the year that Hawaii, New York, Alaska, and Washington legalized abortion. In 1970, the attorneys filed a lawsuit on behalf of Jane Roe along with all other women who either were pregnant or might be pregnant and wanted to consider other options for terminating the pregnancy.

Now, let's discuss the legacy of Roe V. Wade. Even though Roe maintained a low profile after the court sided and ruled in her favor, during the 1980s, she became active in the movement for abortion rights. After Roe became friends with the head of the anti-abortion group and converted to Catholicism, she turned into a vocal opponent of the procedure. After Roe V. Wade, multiple states together imposed all sorts of restrictions in order to weaken abortion rights, and Americans stayed divided over support for a woman's right to choose whether she wants to have or discard the baby.

Although the court upheld the central ruling in Roe V. Wade, it still allowed states to further pass on more abortion restrictions if they did not seem to pose an undue burden. After a long fight and struggle, in 2022, the nation's highest court deliberated on Dobbs v Jackson Women's Health Organization which regarded the constitutionality of a Mississippi law banning almost all abortions after 15 weeks of pregnancy. The lower courts ruled that this law was unconstitutional under Roe V.

Wade because, under this, it had been prohibited from banning abortions before 23 weeks.

Following this, the Supreme Court ruled 6-3 and spoke in favor of Mississippi's law. As a result, Roe was overturned after almost 50 years. Now, after laying out all the facts and figures, it's apparent that women have been once again silenced unfairly. As a matter of fact, numerous women worldwide are still fighting to gain their justified right to abortion. The ongoing protests and riots are proof enough of how things won't settle down easily or quickly. In my opinion, I fully support the fact that it is entirely up to a woman whether she wants to conceive the baby or abort it.

After all, a generalized opinion cannot be made in this regard. People commit crimes, women get raped, have non-serious one-night stands, and sometimes in unfortunate circumstances, such decisions are necessary. My question to all those who disregard this right of a woman is would you have the same stance if a man wanted the same? As odd as it sounds, if you take the time to really think about it, there was a magical role reversal where men would get pregnant and choose not to have the baby, and the ruling would be made in their favor.

All in all, men have always been given a higher preference and importance over women. It is deeply saddening to constantly be hit with the realization of how even centuries later, the world has not progressed enough to give a woman the rights she deserves. All other advancements hold zero value when we fail to understand, care about, and acknowledge the never-ending struggles a woman goes through.

Nowadays, family planning is a core topic of discussion among couples. They wait, analyze, and plan as to when they are ready and willing to bring a child into this world. There's no denying that having a child is a massive responsibility. Thus, preventive measures are taken, and so much thought goes into the process. Similarly, why is it considered immoral, unethical, and downright wrong for a woman as an individual to choose when she is ready to become a mother? Over centuries, abortion has mostly been viewed from an extremely narrow and shallow perspective.

Women are ridiculed, mocked, abused, and even killed for talking about abortion. In the blink of an eye, their essence of womanhood is taken away, and they are belittled to the point of self-hate. Their abilities to become a mother are questioned left, right, and center. Their rights are snatched away as if they never belonged to them. To say that women are ill-treated and shamed when they voice out their preferences regarding the topic at hand would be an understatement.

The million-dollar question is "where are we, as a nation, headed if we continue to follow these backward, ignorant, and insensible practices?" We cannot stop fighting for our rights and the mindsets; we need to keep at it and continue to voice our right to our own bodies.

Key Takeaway:

I, along with numerous other women, strongly condemn anti-abortion laws and practices. Each woman, at any age or time, has the full right to choose when she wants to become a mother. That is a right that should not be taken away by any means. In fact, that right is equivalent to breathing air. It is because of these anti-abortion movements that women fearfully resort to dark and hidden ways to live on their own terms. It's time we truly progress and broaden our perspectives. It's time we see women for who they are instead of dictating what they should or should not do.

"Embolden Women: Unapologetically Me"

Chapter 11: Tips to Empower Women

While it's easy to say women should empower other women, this goal is often left unattained for various reasons. However, if we are to truly succeed in fostering a change for ourselves and other women, we must join hands and unite as one. Only then will we be able to achieve gender equality and live freely on our own terms. So, have you ever wondered what empowering women looks like in day-to-day life, especially for other women?

We have surely come a long way on the road to gender equality. Yet sometimes, it feels like progress has come to a halt. Women still take up fewer positions as CEOs; the gender pay gap exists; men continue to dictate terms to women; women's voices are unheard; all kinds of abuse persist, etc. Therefore, keeping these factors in mind, there's still a long way to go.

But the great news is that there's a massive power in collective action. In today's time and age, women are far more revved up and connected to each other than before. In fact, women supporting other women is HUGE, as it speaks to and nourishes one of the most foundational aspects of who we are as feminine beings. It is our nature to gather and sustain each other.

Even though each woman is a powerful force, our power is multiplied when we are united in sisterhood. So, without further ado, let's strive to lead the movement for large-scale gender equality, comprehend how women can support one another daily, and hold our heads high.

Ways women can empower themselves and each other:

1. Validate self-expression: Unsurprisingly, women's narratives are largely underrepresented in the media and popular culture. So, the next time you see a woman taking it upon herself to share her story and let herself be vulnerable, make sure to acknowledge that act of bravery. Make it a point to let her know you see her, hear her, and honor her truth. If you see another person putting down a woman's personal experience or bullying her, step in and gently remind them that this is her truth, and you applaud her for speaking up about it.

2. Check assumptions at work: Simply identifying as a woman doesn't preclude you from bias or automatically translate to you being free from responsibility when it comes to the oppression of others. Therefore, it's essential to recognize your unconscious biases against other women based on their age, race, gender expression, sexual orientation, body type, physical abilities, or socioeconomic background. It's highly essential to check your own unconscious biases and uplift the voices of other women of color in your field who face additional biases in the workplace. Unconscious biases often lead to systemic discrimination. The first step in addressing this issue is checking your own beliefs and encouraging the discussion of biases in your workplace when you notice a lack of diversity and inclusivity.

3. Compliment the mind and soul instead of only the body: Women get several compliments about their physical appearance, but what matters is that they also get appreciated for other things such as their intellect, personality, soul, etc.

4. Offer genuine support: Some people appear to be strong and have it all together. They're thriving in their personal and professional life on the outside, but we should never assume everything is picture-perfect. There is always more than what meets the eye. Therefore, offering support to strong women should not be undermined. In fact, women from certain ethnicities often feel burdened by the need to portray a very strong image, even though they're far more at risk of mental illnesses such as anxiety, OCD, and depression. Not making assumptions or having theories about which female needs help is a key part of offering genuine support. Take out time to check up-close on all the women in your life and let them know they are cared for.

5. Prioritize solitude: Women are usually trained to prioritize other people's needs before their own. One guaranteed way of empowering yourself and other women is by encouraging and validating alone time. We often forget the significance of unplugging and separating ourselves from others to reflect on what's happening in our lives. Alone time/ me-time is not only great for your overall well-being, but it can also increase the quality of the relationships you have with other women. So, take out time to reinvigorate your mind and body. Simultaneously, you should also encourage other women to schedule alone time and encourage them to prioritize solitude. We all need to recharge ourselves, and what better way to do that than this.

6. Support whisper networks that benefit other women: We are all looking for the next best thing. But ensuring other women have access to the same beneficial information is crucial in empowering women. It's highly imperative for women to take on the mantle of disseminating intel to each other that can assist them in succeeding in their careers. Learn to share your experiences in secure, trusted networks of other women and give them insight into how you achieved something. Take the initiative to warn others to avoid bad things you experienced, extending support and guidance.

7. Invest in women-owned businesses: Running a business is no easy task, and women who own/run businesses are continuously shortchanged. Males raise more money than their female counterparts. Thus, go out of your way to encourage and support female businesses, as most lack adequate support. Choose to invest your time or money in competent, capable women who are making a good impact.

8. Subvert gender norms around children: There are numerous examples of how gender socialization starts at birth. Boys are encouraged to explore the environment, whereas girls are made to worry about getting their hands dirty. Parents must make offsetting these gender roles a priority, be role models for young girls, and pay close attention to common statements about gender behavior.

Move away from the stereotypical phrases and activities that differentiate the genders and encourage girls to be brave and experiment.

9. Avoid unnecessary competition with other women: While competition is healthy, it may also be unnecessary and toxic in some cases. Therefore, I urge women to stop unhealthy competition. There's no need to be vindictive or unfair. Always remember that dimming someone else's light will never make you shine brighter.

10. Go out of your way to make other women feel good: Usually, women don't get the appreciation and kindness they deserve. They are under heavy pressure to adhere to unrealistic standards of beauty and social behaviors. So, speak a kind word or two. Voice out how they are doing a fantastic job. There's no need to feel shy, even with strangers. After all, we are all women and easily relate to each other in so many things.

11. Assist women in making time for themselves: It's vital to reinforce the fact that we women need time to slow down and indulge in self-care. If you have the golden opportunity to assist any of your friends or family, think of it as a means of their prayers being answered through you. Some examples are as follows: helping with chores, picking up a friend/sister's kids from school, scheduling a massage or spa treatment, or just giving someone the time to pause and refuel. Assisting other women is a splendid way to be of service to the ones we love.

12. Bring women into the conversation: In business meetings, men are often the ones who do most of the talking. Before a meeting, approach a colleague and give them the confidence to speak up. As a result, she will be prepared for the ask, and her value will be demonstrated.

13. Partnering with male allies: Empowering women should not be limited to women alone; men can empower women as well by being true allies and having enough education to not create the barrier in the first place. This fight is not for women alone; it's a fight both men and women need to fight against patriarchy hand in hand. It's not only for women to empower other women, but we also need men allies who are taking the baton for women's empowerment. Most of the techniques applied to women in this book can very well be leveraged by men to empower and support women in their life. Fathers, brothers, husbands, significant others, bosses, male colleagues, male teachers, and many more can play a significant role in uplifting and emboldening the women in their lives.

As a man, if you've cared for any woman in your life, call out men in your circles with predatory tendencies/behavior, break your bro codes, and let that woman sitting next to you finish her sentence without anyone else cutting her off – and if they do cut her off, tell them to shut up and let her finish – give them equal opportunities, and do all of the things I have mentioned in the above pointers without making it feel like you are doing them a favor. The best male allies are the ones who really acknowledge patriarchy, who don't get defensive, and who realize that they may be, are trying to be different but are still benefiting from patriarchy in some ways. If you are a man reading this book, know that you have to use your great power with great responsibility.

"Embolden Women: Unapologetically Me"

Conclusion

I want to challenge all my readers to dream big. If your dreams don't scare you, they are not big enough. We need to ask ourselves if we are living our life unapologetically, according to our own terms, and not according to the ones set by others in the name of culture, tradition, norm, or religion. Do we have the freedom to choose and live as we please? This question has no right or wrong answer. What is right for one person may not necessarily be right for another.

For example, I am passionate about my career, and I would do anything to keep that a priority; that is my right, and I should not feel guilty about it. There are also women who are homemakers and full-time mothers, and that is their choice and their right. Regardless of what you choose, what matters is whether you are happy or whether you feel trapped or lost. As working women, we face challenges because of established norms, culture, beliefs, etc. All of us must find work-life balance and learn to deal with challenges, especially women from eastern cultures.

Having too many boundaries and expectations puts women in a disadvantaged position, and it's about time we break free of the chains that hold us back. We need to learn to stand our ground without feeling guilty and challenge the traditional norms. There is no need to accept limitations set by others as long as we believe in who we are. A happy woman keeps her family happy. How can we inspire our children if we don't take a stance on our aspirations and goals? Our children are constantly learning from us and looking up to us.

They will likely follow and preach what they see us do. The question is, if we can't do it ourselves, how can anyone else do it for us? To live a life on one's own terms, without limitations, is what it means to be "Unapologetically Me." Let's not wait for our significant other to give us permission to live. Let's enjoy life freely and chase our dreams. As women, we seem to spend half of our lives pleasing the men in our lives because we are subtly taught that from an early age. We do this due to our subconscious cultural bias, which makes us do so without even realizing how much we're being subdued.

Instead of fanciful tales about a prince charming coming to the rescue, we need to teach our girls about tales of self-reliant women with a strong will to survive without inhibition. As women, let's commit to supporting and lifting one another up regardless of race or religion. Women showing support and sustaining one another can be very powerful. Let's unite as one womanhood. Let's share our stories and encourage every woman to feel free to be herself; it's OKAY to be vulnerable; it's brave to share your personal story with others.

Let us honor those women who are and have been brave enough to share their truth. Let's look past our looks and learn to praise each other on our accomplishments, kindness, strength, dedication, courage, and learning. We must let go of our unconscious biases and uplift other women, especially those of color and minorities.

We need to have discussions openly, encouraging one another to overcome our biases and help one another. Let's use our voices and abilities to boost other women at work, school, and in our social circles. Let's celebrate other women's achievements without bias and questioning. Let's strive to empower other women by putting them in the spotlight.

We should build reliable networks and channels for women to share their experiences of abuse, bias, harassment, and so forth. The higher rate of depression in women is due to the fact that many women don't realize they are victims of emotional abuse. Let's help one another to learn about harassment, bias, and emotional abuse. With greater awareness, multiple women worldwide can be saved and can develop the courage to remove themselves from a toxic equation.

Finally, let's all **Embolden ourselves and be truly Unapologetic about who we are**; we don't need to justify our actions and behaviors to others. It's enough that we do something because we want to. We don't need to convince others to understand. It is our right to make a choice, and it must be made without any justification.

It is time to learn to live guilt-free and to be a role model for young women and girls, accepting proudly that **WE ARE FEMINISTS AND WE EMPOWER OTHER WOMEN!**

"Embolden Women: Unapologetically Me"

Made in the USA
Monee, IL
05 November 2022

17173400R00103